THE LEADERSHIP LIBRARY

VOLUME 16

THE HEALTHY HECTIC HOME

Other books in THE LEADERSHIP LIBRARY

Well-Intentioned Dragons by Marshall Shelley

Liberating the Leader's Prayer Life by Terry Muck

Clergy Couples in Crisis by Dean Merrill

When It's Time to Move by Paul D. Robbins, ed.

Learning to Lead by Fred Smith

What Every Pastor Needs to Know about Music, Youth, and Education
   by Garth Bolinder, Tom McKee, and John Cionca

Helping Those Who Don't Want Help by Marshall Shelley

Preaching to Convince by James D. Berkley, ed.

When to Take a Risk by Terry Muck

Weddings, Funerals, and Special Events
   by Eugene Peterson, Calvin Miller, and others

Making the Most of Mistakes by James D. Berkley

Leaders by Harold Myra, ed.

Being Holy, Being Human, by Jay Kesler

Secrets of Staying Power, by Kevin Miller

The Magnetic Fellowship, by Larry Weeden, ed.

THE LEADERSHIP LIBRARY

Volume
16

The Healthy Hectic Home

Raising a Family in the Midst of Ministry

Marshall Shelley

Carol Stream, Illinois

WORD PUBLISHING
Dallas · London · Sydney · Singapore

THE HEALTHY HECTIC HOME

©1988 Christianity Today, Inc.

A LEADERSHIP/Word Book. Copublished by Christianity Today, Inc. and Word, Inc. Distributed by Word Books.

Cover art by Joe Van Severen

The historical vignettes in Chapter 1 were adapted by permission from *Martin Luther Had a Wife* (Tyndale, 1983) and *Catherine Marshall Had a Husband,* by William J. Petersen (Tyndale, 1986).

Unless otherwise indicated, Scripture quotations are from The New International Version of the Bible (NIV), copyright © 1978 The New York International Bible Society. Used by permission of Zondervan Bible Publishers. Where the Good News Bible (GNB) is indicated, quotations are from Today's English Version of the Bible, copyright © 1966, 1971, 1976 American Bible Society. Used by permission.

Library of Congress Cataloging-in-Publication Data

Shelley, Marshall.
    The healthy hectic home.

    (The Leadership library ; v. 16)
      1. Clergymen's families.
I. Title.   II. Series.
BV4396.S55   1988   248.8'92   88-22296
ISBN 0-917463-21-8

Printed in the United States of America

89801239   AGF   987654321

To Susan,
my partner in ministry,
in marriage,
in family life,
and in trying to balance all three.

CONTENTS

INTRODUCTION

Home is the seminary of all other institutions.

E. H. Chapin

Ask virtually anyone with children at home to describe family life in one word, and you'll rarely hear a word like *placid, quiet,* or *still.*

Instead, the word is almost always *busy, hurried,* or even *chaotic.*

The homes of pastors and other church leaders are not immune from the tempo of the twentieth century. If anything, they feel the busyness even more. Everyone in the pastor's family is likely to be actively involved, not only at school and in the community, but also at church.

A pastor's home is not a contemplative retreat; it's a barely contained whirlwind. (As a colleague of mine loves to say amid the daily rush and tumble, "Tempest et fugeting all over.") What's the effect of this kind of home? How does the ministry affect the pastor's family? And how does the pastor's family life affect the ministry?

With both Jesse James and James Dobson the sons of ministers, it's difficult to generalize about the effects of growing up in a ministry-centered home. But pastors care about the effect their vocation has upon their offspring. How can pastors help make both their family life and their church life pleasing to God?

Is it possible to have a healthy, hectic home?

The goal of this book is not to rehash common Christian wisdom about child rearing or marriage enrichment. Principles for raising kids and loving your spouse can be found in abundance in bookstores and on video tapes, and most of it applies to ministry families as much as to anyone else.

Nor does the book simply expose the eccentricities of selected ministry families around the country. My aim is to find the common elements that virtually all pastors' families experience — the special advantages and difficulties of a ministry home — and to show how different families are trying to maximize the advantages and overcome the difficulties in raising a healthy family.

To this end, LEADERSHIP Journal surveyed more than one thousand pastors and pastors' spouses. The results provide much of the basis for this book, and specific quotations from the survey responses are sprinkled throughout the chapters to illustrate the findings.

While this book focuses on the families of pastors, most of the principles easily transfer to the families of anyone who is "ministry minded." Pastoral families aren't the only ones whose lives revolve around the church. Active lay people — Sunday school superintendents, board members, committee chairpersons, key teachers, and lay volunteers — may also find their thoughts centered on church activities, their personal calendars dominated by church events, and their children considering the church their second home. Such families have much in common with the pastor's, so they also stand to benefit from the insights and experiences offered in this book.

I need to offer a few words about the survey on which this book is based. Those surveyed represented a cross section of urban (20 percent), suburban (29 percent), small-town (41 percent), and rural (10 percent) churches. The average Sunday morning attendance of those churches also represented the diversity typical today:

Less than 100 (27 percent)

100–199 (28 percent)
200–299 (16 percent)
300–499 (12 percent)
500–999 (10 percent)
More than 1,000 (7 percent).

The pastors and spouses represented all age groups from 20 to 69. About 11 percent had no children. The children of the other 89 percent were of various ages:

29 percent had children under 5 years old
38 percent had children between 5 and 12
23 percent had children between 13 and 17
39 percent had children 18 or older.

As you will see in the pages to follow, the respondents offered candid observations about the joys and pains of life in a ministry home. The pastor's home is not always idyllic. And yet on the LEADERSHIP survey, the ministry home was considered generally a good place to enjoy family life.

When pastors were asked, *Which of the following best typifies how you generally feel about your family life: Very positive, positive, somewhat negative, very negative?* 84 percent said *positive* or *very positive*. Only 16 percent felt somewhat negative or very negative. Surprisingly, pastors' spouses were even more positive (93 percent indicating positive or very positive feelings).

But great challenges face a pastor's family. Pastors surveyed were asked to "check all that apply," and the results were:

Time pressure — 83 percent
Dealing with congregational expectations — 53 percent
Building a better relationship with my spouse — 53 percent (slightly fewer pastors' spouses — 45 percent — checked this one)
Building a better relationship with my children — 50 percent (again, fewer spouses — 38 percent — felt this was a great challenge)
Raising a moral family in an immoral age — 46 percent
Misbehavior by a family member — 13 percent
Being accepted by the congregation — 12 percent (in this

case, *more* spouses — 30 percent — said this was a challenge)

Being accepted by the community — 9 percent (again, pastors' spouses differed with 16 percent).

When forced to choose the *one* greatest challenge, pastors pointed to time pressure (48 percent), congregational expectations (20 percent), building a better relationship with my spouse (15 percent), and building a better relationship with my children (5 percent).

Pastors' spouses had a slightly different order: time pressure (46 percent), congregational expectations (18 percent), raising a moral family in an immoral age (9 percent), and building a better relationship with my spouse (7 percent).

Such were the primary concerns of the ministers and spouses surveyed.

Throughout this book, you'll notice virtually all the illustrations emerge out of families in which the pastor is male. We recognize the growing number of female pastors, yet fewer than 4 percent of our surveys were returned by female pastors or their spouses. More research needs to be done on the unique dynamics of this type of pastoral family. Because of the limited information currently available, this book leans primarily on the experiences of "the pastor and his wife."

In addition to surveying ministry families, I interviewed dozens of pastors and grown children of pastors. Some of their stories have been camouflaged to protect the privacy of those involved, but they all reflect the actual experiences of families in ministry.

A few years ago, one of the editors of *Who's Who* was reportedly asked, "How can a person get his name into your listings?" His answer: "It helps to be born into a Methodist parsonage." His point was that a disproportionate number of achievers come from clergy homes.

It *is* possible to have a healthy home, even when the family schedule is hopelessly intertwined with the church calendar. I trust the stories and reflections in this book will help you make the most of your church life and develop a healthy, even if chronically hectic, home.

ONE

FAITHFUL BUT NOT FLAWLESS

Spiritual leadership begins at home. In dealing with the family, remember that you have been blessed by the Lord, not beatified. Don't expect them to stop asking you to carry out the garbage.

PAUL W. CARLSON

What is a healthy, hectic home? What does one look like?

Consider these four snapshots from ministry families, three of them historic, one contemporary.

Despite appearances, being a Christian leader does not eliminate family strife. Husband-and-wife arguments over ministry issues are at least as old as Moses and Zipporah.

William and Catherine Booth, for instance, founders of The Salvation Army, were both highly opinionated. Before their marriage, Catherine set four rules to govern their relationship: (1) never have secrets; (2) never have separate purses; (3) talk out differences to secure harmony rather than pretend differences don't exist; (4) never argue in front of the children.

The fact that two of the four refer directly to differences of opinion is not insignificant. Only eight months into their marriage, Catherine wrote a letter to a friend, praising her husband's preaching: "My precious William excelled himself and electrified the people. You would indeed have participated in my joy and pride could you have heard and seen what I did. Bless the Lord, O my soul."

The next paragraph, however, was written with bolder, less refined, penmanship: "I have just come into the room where my dear wife is writing this precious document and, snatching the paper, have read the above eulogistic sentiments. I just want to say that this very same night she gave me a certain lecture on my blockheadism, stupidity, etc., and lo, she writes to you after this fashion. However, she is an increasingly precious treasure to me, despite the occasional dressing down."

Has there ever existed a ministry family that didn't lament the heavy time demands? More than four hundred years ago, Martin and Katherine Luther struggled with his need to be gone so much.

Once while he was traveling, Luther wrote home: "To the saintly, worrying Lady Katherine Luther, doctor at Zulsdorf [the home of her inherited farm] and Wittenberg, my gracious, dear wife. We thank you heartily for being so worried that you can't sleep, for since you started worrying about us, a fire broke out near my door, and yesterday, no doubt due to your worry, a big stone, save for the angels, would have fallen and crushed me like a mouse in a trap. If you don't stop worrying, I'm afraid the earth will swallow us. Pray, let God worry."

Katie, at times, also struggled with Martin's presence. He would often have students around the dinner table, plying him with questions and taking notes, while Katie would sit at the far end surrounded by the children. When she found out the students intended to publish their notes, she wanted to charge them for their note-taking privileges. Martin refused. Eventually the students published 6,596 entries in their various versions of *Table Talks*. If Katie had had her way, she would have had a guilder for each.

Martin's sense of humor was often called on in domestic situations. "I would not exchange Katie for France or Venice," he said, although once, after Katie had contradicted him in front of dinner guests, he said, "If I should ever marry again, I should hew myself an obedient wife out of stone."

But Martin deeply valued family life. Before his marriage, he sometimes spoke of matrimony as a necessity for the flesh. Afterward, he saw it as an opportunity for the spirit. And he often quoted the saying, "Let the wife make her husband glad to come home, and let him make her sorry to see him leave." Separation only increased Martin and Katherine's appreciation of a healthy home.

Most ministry families have a love/hate relationship with sermon preparation. They realize how essential — and how demanding — it is. And they often find themselves playing a part, intentionally or otherwise, in a sermon's development, as Susie Spurgeon, wife of the prominent London pulpiteer, discovered late one night.

Charles Spurgeon would finish preparing his sermons on Saturday night. One evening things did not go well. He mulled over a text for hours. He had consulted commentaries, prayed, jotted down ideas that didn't go anywhere, and now was becoming frustrated. "I was as much distressed as he was," said Susie, "but I could not help him. . . . At least, I thought I could not."

Finally, Susie urged him to go to bed. She would wake him at dawn. He would be able to think more clearly then.

But during the night, Susie heard him talking in his sleep. She listened. It wasn't gibberish. "Soon I realized that he was going over the subject . . . and was giving a clear and distinct exposition of its meaning with much force and freshness. . . . If I could but seize and remember the salient points, he would have no difficulty in developing and enlarging upon them."

She lay in bed, "repeating over and over again the chief points," and fell asleep about the time she was supposed to waken Charles.

When he awoke and noticed the time, he was irritated. "You promised to waken me very early. See the time! Why did you let me sleep? I don't know what I'm going to do this morning."

Then Susie told him what had happened during the night and repeated to him the main points he had made in his sleep.

"You mean I preached that in my sleep?" He could hardly believe it. "That is just what I wanted. That's the true explanation of the text." From the explanation Susie furnished, Charles went into the pulpit and preached a powerful sermon.

Little wonder, then, that when missionary David Livingstone once asked Spurgeon, "How do you manage to do two men's work in a single day?" without a pause, Charles responded, "You have forgotten that there are two of us, and the one you see the least of often does the most work" — a response that could be echoed a great number of pastors' homes today.

More recently, Episcopal rector John Yates of The Falls Church in Falls Church, Virginia, tells a story that shows how family life can directly affect the worship hour itself:

"Young children don't take Communion in our congregation, but they do come to the rail, kneel, and receive a blessing from the pastor (in this case, me). When my twin daughters were four years old, they came to the rail, and I laid my hands on the first and quietly began to recite, 'Susie, may the Lord bless you and keep you . . .' Other people were kneeling nearby during this reverent moment.

"In the midst of my blessing, she suddenly exclaimed loudly, 'Daddy, I'm Libby, not Susie!' The whole congregation looked up, startled, and then burst out laughing.

"Afterward the senior warden, the man who heads our board, said to my wife, 'I know we expect John to work hard, but I think we need to help him find more time to be with his family.' "

What can we make of these brief snapshots of life in ministry homes?

We immediately recognize that ministry families are not flawless. But flawed doesn't necessarily mean unhealthy. The goal of ministry-oriented homes is not perfection but faithfulness.

Another fact that quickly emerges is that healthy ministry families don't all look alike. If anything is clear in the results of the research for this book, it's that there is no single, right way to structure family life in ministry. The models are as diverse as the personalities of each parent and child. This book reflects the diversity of roles and strategies developed by today's pastoral families. But two things they share: a commitment to minister and a commitment to build a healthy home.

Gigi Tchividjian, who grew up in a ministry home as the daughter of Billy Graham, tells about a conversation with her 4-year-old son in which they were discussing what a home was. His conclusion: "A home is a place where you come in out of the rain."

That's not a bad definition for any home, but for ministry families, it's the essential goal: to make the home a place of security, warmth, and reassurance — not only for the members of the congregation, but for family members as well. The following chapters point the way to that kind of ministry home.

TWO
PASTORAL PERKS

If you wish to leave much wealth to your children, leave them in God's care. Do not leave them riches, but virtue and skill. For if they learn to expect riches, they will not mind anything besides, and their abundant riches shall give them the means of screening the wickedness of their ways.

JOHN CHRYSOSTOM

What are the advantages of raising a family in a pastor's home?

A couple of years ago, I had the chance to sit down with James Dobson, perhaps the best-known champion of the family in the contemporary Christian world, and ask him about his days as a preacher's kid. I was curious whether his experiences in the church were positive or negative.

His reply: "Very positive. The church was the center of our social life, and I felt loved and accepted by this extended 'family.' That little body of believers provided an unshakable foundation of values and understanding, which I still hold firmly today. I was three years old when I voluntarily knelt and gave my heart to the Lord, and I'm still grateful for the teachings I received in those early years."

Church life, however, has changed dramatically in the last generation. What about the differences between the family life he experienced growing up in a small church in Oklahoma and family life in the large Southern California congregation he's involved in now? Is the small church or the large church more conducive to family life?

"Each has its own contribution to make," Dobson replied. "Some people thrive better in a crowd, and they need the programs and specialists that can be provided only in a large church community. Adolescents, for example, are driven by this 'urge to herd,' and they feel more secure with larger numbers of their peers.

"On the other hand, some people need the intimacy and personal touch of a small church family. In my own life, it was this sense of being known and cared for in a small church that hooked me into the fellowship. The warmth I felt there compensated for the lack of sophistication in program and personnel."

Whether in a large or small church, pastors find that there are distinct advantages to raising a family in a ministry home. Here are some of the perks identified in the survey.

Flexible Hours

The first advantage many pastoral families mention is a flexible work schedule.

"I never missed one of my son's soccer games," said a pastor from Massachusetts. "The great benefit of a pastor's schedule is that you can juggle appointments, plan to work some nights, and be free in the afternoon to watch soccer. The lawyer, the physician, and the stockbroker couldn't be there, but I was."

A pastor's wife from California said, "I work four days a week outside the home. Usually I have Tuesdays off, so my husband, whose schedule is flexible, can also take Tuesdays as his day off. We spend most Tuesdays at home, although sometimes we go out to eat or play tennis. As I look back, I realize we have had our most serious talks about ourselves, our marriage, the family, and our future on those days. We have worked out more problems during those times than any other. I don't get much 'house' work accomplished, but I do get a lot of 'home' work done."

Spiritual Role Models

One of the survey respondents said, "Children have a model of involved church members in their parents. We constantly have people in our home whom we *want* our kids to know."

A pastor's wife elaborated on this fringe benefit: "Because my husband is a pastor, we've had people in our home whom our children never would have had the benefit of knowing otherwise: African pastors, missionaries to Brazil, evangelists, other preachers. Our kids have been able to talk to them, play games with them, and find out more about the world and what makes people tick."

But there are other spiritual role models for ministry families. Joseph Stowell, prior to becoming president of Moody Bible Institute, was a pastor, the son of a pastor, and the grandson of a pastor. When I asked him about the advantages of his upbringing, he said, "One of my best memories is having great Bible teachers around our dining room table: M. R. DeHaan, Sidlow Baxter, and others. I remember one meal when Frank Logsdon, former pastor of Moody Church, leaned over to me and said, 'God has given you a great daddy.' That stuck with me. I felt like, *My dad's a good guy, an important person.*"

Sometimes the role models weren't those you would have expected. Chuck Smith, Jr., who also grew up in a ministry home before becoming a pastor himself, said, "My fondest memory is having godly people in our home who were so animated and enthusiastic when they talked about the Lord. Their devotion to the Lord and the ministry made me feel like this was the most important subject in life. One time my dad had been at a pastor's conference and met four colleagues. This was kind of out of character for him, but Dad spontaneously invited them over to the house. It was stimulating to me because they weren't sharing statistics about who had the most people in their churches; they were sharing their common commitment to Christ." That experience was powerful enough to be remembered twenty-five years later.

Often one of the best role models is the pastor himself. Family members see, up close and personal, a person whose life is committed to ministry.

"My son gets to see me at work," said a pastor in New Hampshire. "He gets to share some of the pressure and ethos of LEADERSHIP, and he sees me interact with people in our home. And when I'm able to be vulnerable and transparent, he sees times in my life when I'm both elated and discouraged. Not all children are able to be so close to their parents' vocations."

Richard Strauss, who pastors in Escondido, California, experienced that from the other side as the son of prominent pastor and speaker Lehman Strauss. "I enjoyed the fact that my dad was respected. I mean, here was a man standing in the pulpit teaching the Word of God, and people were listening and writing things down, and their lives were being changed. And that was my dad! I was a retiring child, not outgoing at all. Dad was such a strong personality that he overshadowed those around him. But I didn't resent that. I felt like some of the respect people felt for him trickled down to me. Part of my identity was being his son."

Another pastor's son, now grown, said, "I remember sometimes on the way home from church I would ask my dad a question that perplexed me about the Bible or the church. I remember thinking (though I never would have admitted it to my dad) that it was great to have this kind of exclusive access to him for my questions."

Richard Strauss also remembers: "My dad had his study at home, and one day I walked past his study and heard him talking. I knew there wasn't anybody in there. I thought, *Who's Dad talking to?* So I sat down and listened. He was praying.

"I sat there for ten or fifteen minutes and listened. That was a moving experience, and after that, every once in a while if I knew he was praying, I'd sit outside his door and listen.

That's something that's grown more meaningful now than it was at the time."

Atmosphere

The atmosphere a family experiences in ministry can also be invigorating.

Part of this is simply a natural effect of a ministry environment. "After thirty-four years of married life and three grown children, God has given us a close family, and we didn't really work on it being so," said an Evangelical Free Church pastor. "It seems to be a by-product of intensely living for and serving God. All three children walk with God, love us, and love each other. I love my work as a pastor — and my family could see that and seemed to benefit from that."

Another part of this is due to the experiences any pastor has. "In our counseling, we learn from others who have made mistakes," said a Lutheran pastor in Iowa. "From being involved in so many other family situations, I gain insights for my own family."

In addition, the atmosphere of the worshiping community can have a positive effect. Preacher's-kid-turned-preacher Joe Stowell tells the story: "When my own children started coming along, I asked my dad, 'Why do you think all three of your children went into the ministry?'

" 'I don't know,' he said. 'Your mother and I can't take credit for it. We think it's because the church in Hackensack, New Jersey, consistently prayed for you children. In prayer meetings, people would pray aloud for you by name.'

"I attribute that to the fact that my behavior drove 'em to their knees," Joe said with a laugh. "But I do think as pastors' kids, we may have more prayer poured into our lives than other kids."

In addition, the surveys revealed other atmospheric elements in a ministry home that benefit a family.

"We share in the love some parishioners have for their pastor. While we've suffered from some of the 'alligators' in the church, people with ego problems, our family has greatly benefited from the love of caring people."

"We have lots of people willing to baby-sit and be 'grandparents' for our kids. They give special attention to PK's."

"The church body provides a good moral climate."

"We enjoy a spiritual atmosphere within the home that is lived on a practical, day-to-day basis. My children not only play 'school,' they also play 'church.' At least at this point in their lives, they appreciate the role of pastor."

"We have plenty of exposure to books that enrich the home."

"Because of our involvement at church, it's easier to talk about our faith and values."

A number of pastors' wives identified teamwork with their husbands as one of the joys of being a pastor's wife. Not many professions allow the entire family to share work to the degree a pastor's family can share ministry — seeing one another working, contributing to the common cause.

These atmospheric conditions are conducive to growing a healthy family.

More Than the Material World

Finances are commonly seen as a drawback to life in ministry. But often it's not the salary itself that causes problems; it's the contrast with the rest of the congregation. The pastor's salary is usually on the low side of the congregational bell curve.

This creates some unusual pressures. Despite their more modest income, the pastor's family is expected to dress as well, give the kids as many opportunities, dine out as often, and entertain as often or more so than more affluent parishioners. There's pressure to join in the expensive activities.

"We can manage our money to meet our needs, but we're surrounded by affluence in which we cannot share," one pastor said.

Pastors, by and large, seem able to handle the disparity

reasonably well. It's a greater challenge for their families. "My voluntary vow of poverty becomes my family's involuntary vow of poverty," says New England pastor Henry Brinton. An Alban Institute study found that half the clergy spouses polled had a major concern about finances. It appears that wives are often more concerned about finances than their husbands are.

Pastor's wife Mary Bouma reflects on why wives may feel more pressure than pastors: "Perhaps it's because we have more of an appreciation for nice things. Probably it's because we're forced to spend a lot of our time working with material things. It usually falls to us to decorate the house and keep it clean, plan the family wardrobes and keep them in repair. So it is part of our job to work with possessions, and it is often hard not to desire nicer ones, especially when people all around us have things nicer than ours."

Children of the parsonage can also feel the pinch. Tim Stafford, who grew up the son of a Presbyterian minister, observed, "A pastor's kids grow up surrounded by people who have slightly nicer cars and bigger houses than they do. Money to a kid, in case you've forgotten, conveys status. When you're fourteen, status is virtually all there is."

Despite the financial pressures, a significant number of survey respondents indicated the emphasis on spiritual priorities outweighed the money problems. The entire family learns quickly and clearly that there is more to life than material goods.

"Our kids see actual ministry going on all the time. And because we're on support status in a church-planting situation, they're learning early to trust God and to pray for our needs," said a pastor's wife from California.

Another pastor's wife said, "Our children have experienced what many youngsters today miss: they learned they couldn't have everything they wanted while growing up. This has enabled them to go without their 'wants' if there wasn't enough money to provide them."

Businessman Fred Smith was raised in a pastor's home in

the inner city of Nashville, Tennessee. He recalls the lasting impression it made on him.

"Most pastors' families, I suspect, face squarely the constant juxtaposition of the spiritual and the material. Ours certainly did. Our home existed for the spiritual welfare of the church. I never heard business discussed, for example, until I left home at age 21. I had to gain all my business knowledge as an adult (and felt envious of the children of executives — just as those who come to Christ later in life often envied us preachers' kids our Bible knowledge).

"And yet, the material side of life was a continual struggle. When I asked why our family didn't eat in restaurants more often, Dad would say, 'A minister's family makes certain sacrifices. Eating out is not bad. But our family is centered on spiritual things, not material.' As kids, we always knew heaven was as real to Mom and Dad as earth."

Making the financial situation an advantage or a drawback hinges on the parents' attitude. Again, Tim Stafford reflects: "Pastors' kids often feel poor. Sometimes they pick up those feelings from their parents, who tend to be well-educated, ambitious, verbal people who might make more money in other jobs. Some parents, conscious of their sacrifice, mention it. Their children, who may not recall a word of the good spiritual counsel they are getting, remember the remarks about money.

"As a child, I was reasonably normal, and I felt our lack of status. But, remarkably enough, I never felt that we were truly poor. . . . I can remember the many times I had to get out to push the old car out of the parking space — it didn't go into reverse, and we had no money to pay a mechanic. But I cannot remember ever feeling poor."

The key, Stafford says, was his parents' aggressive posture: Instead of talking about their lack, they focused on what they had. They tried to help their kids believe they were enjoying the finest things of life: books, music, camping, baseball games. "We thought we were better off than people who had to buy big cars and steaks to enjoy life.

"Giving helped, too. An early, vivid memory of mine is of my mother late one night writing out checks to various Christian organizations. 'Tithing makes me feel so rich,' she said to me as she looked up. 'We have all this money to give away.' "

It was her attempt, a successful attempt, to tranform the material side of ministry from a drawback to a definite benefit.

Relocation

Like those in the military, families in ministry face the distinct possibility, even likelihood, of frequent relocation. This is often cited as a drawback to life in the ministry. As one survey respondent said, "Frequent moves make it hard to maintain close friendships." Others pointed to the sense of rootlessness felt by children who have moved often. When they go to college and people ask where they're from, they're at a loss. They usually respond with the place where their parents currently live, even when that place doesn't feel like home.

A pastor's wife described a vivid impression: "My husband recently accepted a call that meant moving all the way across the country. Since we had been in our previous church twelve years, our twelve-year-old had never known another home. When we began to consider positions in different parts of the country, it all sounded exciting to her. She was cheerful throughout the move and settling into the new house and school.

"The first clue that things might not be as they appeared came a week later when I helped her hang her mirror. She insisted on having each piece of furniture exactly the way it had been in her previous room. When I asked why, she answered that she had read in a magazine article that this was one way to minimize the trauma of a move. I found it rather poignant that this child, who was only beginning to emerge from little girlhood, was matter-of-factly setting about to 'minimize her trauma.' "

But while this area, like finances, may be a disadvantage in some ways, in other ways it is seen by many pastoral families as an advantage.

When moves are contemplated, pastors are able to weigh the impact upon their families. They often have some choice in the matter of location. In the LEADERSHIP survey, 77 percent of pastors said that family considerations entered into their accepting a call to a particular church. Some of the factors included being near extended family, a particular school setting, job opportunities for the pastor's spouse, and families in the area with children approximately the ages of the pastor's children.

Some pastoral families have sacrificed salary and the prestige of a larger congregation for other factors that would help their families.

"We left our church in the Chicago suburbs and moved to a smaller church here in New Hampshire," said one pastor, "because I didn't like what the suburbs were doing to our 8- and 10-year-old. We would give them $3 a week allowance. Their friends at school would get $20 a week. Their friends were into designer clothes and 'sleep-overs' that usually included a violent horror movie on video. They made anyone with different values feel outcast.

"Plus," said the pastor, "I'm not a city person. All I know to do in the city is go to a museum, a mall, or a movie. Our family enjoys camping, backpacking, canoeing, swimming, skiing. Those have been the settings of our best family moments — when we'd enjoy just talking. It's easier to do those things in our current church. Our move hasn't solved all the problems, of course, but we're much happier here."

One of the advantages of the pastorate: many times it's possible to change locations for the benefit of the family.

A Close Look at God's Work

"My children are exposed to the reality of God's grace in the lives of others," said one pastor. "People share burdens and problems with us, problems they wouldn't share with anyone else. We're able to pray for people, counsel them, and see God work miracles in their lives."

The task of growing spiritually is continually reinforced in a ministry home. Consider these survey responses:

"We're challenged constantly to improve spiritually."

"Everywhere I've been, my presence as the minister's wife has caused people to think of their spiritual condition. Some have taken positive steps toward the Lord. I've been able to have an influence with certain people that I never would have had as a layperson."

In addition, pastors' families are often involved in ministry, which can offer special rewards. One pastor's wife wrote, "Our whole family goes once a week to visit folks in the nursing home. This has multiple blessings: the kids realize the value of older adults and develop more love and respect for them, and they also experience the love that comes from ministry. We all enjoy seeing the faces in the home light up when we arrive."

Jim and Sally Conway, who pastored for many years in Illinois, said, "We recently asked our kids, all of them now grown and living on their own, what they liked best about growing up in a pastor's family. They all said they appreciated their 'insider's perspective' — seeing mom and dad in ministry yet also being real people who got discouraged, angry, and needed forgiveness like anyone else."

Chuck Smith, Jr., said, "One thing I took for granted that I've come to appreciate now that I'm a pastor is the intimacy with God and his Word that our family enjoyed. Our constant orientation was toward God. That's where we sought our solutions; that's how we addressed life. So when I was sick, and there was a period in my childhood when I was sick quite a bit, I just expected my grandmother to put her hand on my forehead and pray for me. I came to expect spiritual ministry as well as medical attention.

"My wife is still somewhat uncomfortable praying aloud. But for me, having grown up this way, praying extemporaneously is a natural expression. I've appreciated the fact that I feel at home in Scripture and in the presence of God. Part of that is due to the environment in which I was raised."

These advantages shine brightly, and it helps to review them, especially when the corresponding disadvantages occasionally cloud our view.

THREE
THE DIFFICULTIES

All happy families resemble each other; each unhappy family is unhappy in its own way.

LEO TOLSTOY

A number of ministry families can identify with the pastor's teenage son who frequently wears a t-shirt imprinted, PROPERTY OF FIRST CHURCH.

"It's the only way I can express the way I feel," he says.

Yes, we must admit that for all the advantages of raising a family in a ministry home, there are also a number of difficulties. When asked about the disadvantages of raising a family in a minister's home, those surveyed offered wide-ranging responses:

"The telephone rings all the time, interrupting our family time."

"My husband is never able to sit with us in worship."

"The uncertainty of your tenure at a church."

"There's exposure to a spiritual atmosphere, but there can also be overexposure to failures of Christians."

"We see the warts of everyone. Everyone sees ours. I strongly identify with the problems of being so close to God's work and close to sin as well."

"Always having to 'be there' — not able to do anything spontaneous on weekends."

"Any trouble I get into with the congregation is magnified

because I'm the pastor. My kids see their dad being attacked, or more likely, they hear from their classmates, 'My parents think your dad really blew it — he got the Smiths really mad at him.' Some pastors' kids have been told, 'Your dad ought to get out of here,' which can be devastating."

"Time pressure limits our opportunities for family events."

"Sunday is NEVER a relaxing day."

Tolstoy said each unhappy family is unhappy in its own way, referring to the tendency of a family to feel its problems are unique. These quotations do show a variety of difficulties, but the bulk of the surveys point to concerns that most ministry families have in common.

Scrutiny by the Saints

Leaders in any field are subject to closer attention and stricter demands. Why do reporters follow the British royal family so closely? Because most Britons (and all tabloid readers) think they own the royal couple. Some people vicariously live out the fairy tale. Others feel it's their *right* to know every move they make since they're supported with public money.

Pastors and their families face some of the same dynamics.

When I asked about the drawbacks of being a pastoral family, one response I often heard was "the sense of continually being watched."

"I usually stand with Mike as he greets people after the service," said a pastor's wife from Milwaukee. "One Sunday we had a guest speaker, and I figured three at the door would be a crowd, so I didn't stand there. One lady rushed up to ask, 'Are you having a fight with your husband?' I never imagined I'd be giving that impression. People really watch!"

Another pastor's wife said, "I didn't realize how closely I was being watched until one lady told me the Sunday after Christmas, 'We can hardly wait till this Sunday each year because we always like to see what your husband gives you for Christmas.' They'd learned my husband enjoys giving clothes."

The effect of this scrutiny varies from family to family. Some enjoy it; others find it tiring. Some see it as a positive influence — a challenge to live up to. Others, however, see it as a temptation: "We're tempted to overemphasize *performing* the Christian life. Because people are looking at us, we sometimes feel we have to be something in public that we may not be in private."

The scrutiny of the saints isn't the only area that pastoral families see as the downside of ministry.

The Holy Family

Not only is the ministry family watched, but many pastoral families feel the observers are looking for something they can't produce. Again and again, those surveyed indicated people expect their family life to be perfect.

"Our children are expected to be model children, to never have any attitude problems. We're supposed to have it all together. But we don't qualify for the holy family."

When it comes to moral behavior, however, pastors' kids can't win: they get less credit for their virtues and more attention for their vices. Whatever they do right, it's "because of the way you were raised." If they do something wrong, the response is, "You, of all people, should know better."

One pastor's son was at a party with his high school friends. When the liquor and drugs came out and the atmosphere started to deteriorate, he decided it was time to leave. As he was thanking the host and saying his farewells, he overheard someone say, "He's leaving because his dad's a preacher."

"That really irritated me," the son said later. "It was *my* decision to leave, but they don't believe that. Anything I do that's right is explained away because of my upbringing."

Another pastor's son, angered at a college classmate, exploded, "All right. I don't drink just because that's what my parents taught me, and you do drink just because that's what your parents allowed. Now can we talk about it intelligently?"

Even involvement in the church is somehow tainted. Some people refuse to believe a pastor's kid would go to church because he actually wants to; surely his parents are forcing him.

Jim Conway remembers that during his pastorate in Illinois, "one of our daughters was in a time of rapid spiritual growth, and she would stand almost every Sunday evening to share something God had been teaching her."

One night after the service, a woman came up to her and said, "We can always count on you to have something to say in the sharing time. Your dad must put you up to it." The daughter did a slow burn.

On the other hand, when the minister's kids are not shining examples of sainthood, that, too, can bring undue attention.

The Conway's daughter Becki remembers an argument in school when a classmate challenged her to back up a particular point of view with Scripture. Becki couldn't.

"You're a preacher's daughter, and you can't even quote the Bible?" the antagonist sneered.

"Well, your dad's a plumber," Becki retorted, "and you don't know how to sweat pipes."

It's a tough situation. When you're 15, you don't want to stand out. It's bad to be too smart and worse to be too good. And when the courageous stands you do take are explained away as the result of parental pressure, there's scant incentive to remain upright.

At Home in Church, Uneasy in the World

One benefit of the pastor's home is familiarity with church life, but the flip side is that the family may feel alienated from the unchurched world. For many in the church, and even more in the outside world, the pastor's family is a peculiar people, more holy than normal, and thus assumed to be uninterested in ordinary human life.

"Our girls sometimes found they weren't invited to friends' parties because 'we know you're a minister's daughter and can't come,' " said Sally Conway. "One woman apologized to me years later for not including me at Tupperware or Avon parties 'because we thought you wouldn't be interested in what we talk about.' "

A number of pastoral families said they deeply appreciated the significance of ministry, but the image of the minister, at least to those outside the church, was something they had to endure. Many preachers' kids said they wanted to live up to the example of their dad's moral character, but they had to live down what other people thought about his profession.

"I admired my dad and my granddad. Many times I thought, *I want to be like them*," said a third-generation pastor. "But I sure had questions about the ministerial image: the schedule, the way people looked at you, the way they thought of you. I didn't want to be holy all the time. I didn't want to cough in a deeper voice."

Another said, "I was fortunate in that Dad was very athletic. He was an all-star football player, and even now he's very active in tennis and water skiing. So I didn't have that image of the pastorate. My resistance was slightly different. I told myself, *I'm gonna be secular. Not profane, but secular. With Christ living in me, I want to be comfortable with non-Christians.* I didn't want to be a minister who was uncomfortable in secular surroundings."

An interesting ambivalence. So many grown children of pastors have deep appreciation for the way they were raised, yet they confess that in school, the pressure from their peers was so great that none was ready to stand up and say, "I am a pastor's kid!" Most of the time they hoped people didn't talk about their dad's vocation. There was profound respect for the man, but embarrassment over the role.

"It's a matter of cultural dissonance," said one pastor's son, now grown and pastoring himself in Southern California. "My comfort zone was inside the subculture of the church. From birth, I've been trained how to act in this environment.

But the outside culture, at least in my upbringing, was presented as so bad, so evil, that I couldn't help but be uncomfortable when I was outside church settings. Any time I heard profanity at school, I'd find myself asking the Lord to forgive me for hearing it. With this overactivated guilt mechanism, I lived a dual life, trying to straddle two cultures.

"I wish I'd understood then that some differences are largely cultural. I've been trying to sensitize our high school Christians to that fact, and it takes some of the stress off. I tell them, 'You don't have to act in a secular culture the way you act in a Christian culture. It's okay not to use Christian vocabulary in a secular culture. What you're doing is almost missionary work. You have to learn cross-cultural communication.' Had I know that in high school, I think I could have existed better with a sense of cultural relevance instead of seeing everything as necessarily a spiritual compromise."

"The term now is *nerd*. I don't know what it was then, maybe *clod* or *square*, but whatever it was, I didn't want to be one," said H. B. London, another pastor who was raised in a pastor's home. "I would do anything not to be square or nerdish — to the point of rejecting many of the things I knew better. As an only child, I didn't have anybody at home who was facing these things with me. So my peer acceptance was not at home; not even at church, because those people didn't matter to me that much. It was at school where it seemed so important that I was accepted. I did not want to be a nerd." And to be the son or daughter of a pastor is, unfortunately, still seen by some as being culturally out of touch.

Perhaps this ambivalence goes back to society's sliding evaluation of the office of pastor. At one time, the ministry was one of the most respected professions. These days, when they rank the prestigious professions, ministers don't even make the list. So family members move from the church, where their relationship with the pastor brings a measure of respect, to the outside culture, where if people find out they're related to a pastor, they tend to be put off.

The Concentration Trap

A person with rigid work hours looks at the pastor's freedom and says, "Boy, I wish I had that flexibility." But the blessing also has its down side. A pastor is never really off duty. A minister can't punch a timecard at 5 P.M. and say, "Well, that's all for today." He's never free of responsibility. The issues of ministry — the next sermon, an upcoming confrontation, a counseling situation — stick in the back of his mind, even when trying to enjoy time with the family.

This can lead to a condition of "physically present but mentally absent." Pastors aren't the only ones afflicted by this condition, of course, but it does seem to be an occupational hazard of ministry.

One pastor's son recalls: "There were several times when Dad and I would be playing catch, enjoying one another's company, and suddenly the phone would ring. Dad would answer, and I'd wait for him to come back out. Sometimes he wouldn't, and the game was over. Other times he'd come back out, and we'd throw the ball some more, but something was different. He was there, but his mind wasn't. I figured it had something to do with the phone call. I came to hate the sound of a telephone ringing. More often than not, it seemed, it cost me my dad."

Feeling Used

Yet another reality of being a pastoral family: being in demand. While that can be affirming, it also has its difficulties.

One pastor said, "My wife struggles with loneliness. The worst part is that whenever someone in the congregation befriends her, she's never sure if it's genuine friendship or if, after a while, the person will say, 'Don't you think we really need to renovate the nursery' (or start a program for the handicapped, or paint the sanctuary, or hire a youth director, or . . .)."

For the pastor's family, it's sometimes hard to know if people genuinely like you or if you're being set up. Even if people aren't actually trying to get something, often members of the pastor's family wonder if they're liked for who they are or for what they represent.

"My wife and I were taken out for a nice dinner and play by a couple in the church," said one pastor. "We thoroughly enjoyed the evening, but within a week, we heard from five different families, 'How was *My Fair Lady*?' or 'I hear you got together with the Lindquists. Aren't they nice folks?' It was obvious the Lindquists had managed to let the word out that they had done something special for the pastor's family."

The pastor concluded, "We felt used. We talked it over and decided that as soon as it becomes apparent that someone is publicizing his 'special relationship' with our family, we won't accept any more invitations from that person."

Some might view that as an oversensitive reaction, but to one degree or another, most pastoral families can easily relate to the feeling of being used.

Making the Most of the Ministry

Randy Pope grew up as the son of a dentist, and as he reflects on his upbringing, he lends some perspective to the experience of ministry families.

"When I was growing up, my father was a dentist. And dentistry, I learned later, is one of the professions with the highest rates of suicide. I don't know all the reasons why, but I can imagine some: you have to take out large loans to get started, you're forced to do precise work in a very confined area (a mouth), you inflict pain and discomfort, people dread seeing you, you're rarely paid promptly.

"But I never heard my dad say anything negative about his profession. I only heard him talk about the benefits: 'Isn't it great that I don't get called in the middle of the night like surgeons do?' 'I'm sure thankful people don't die from dental problems.' 'Dentistry is a great way to help people.' 'I'm really fortunate to be a dentist.' "

Randy says, "As a result of my dad's outlook, there was a time in my adolescence when I wanted to be a dentist, not because I knew anything about it but because my dad had convinced me it was a privilege."

Randy Pope did not become a dentist, however. He's a pastor — at Perimeter Church in Atlanta. But he's trying to do for his children what his father did for him —to show them that the work he does is not a problem but a privilege.

FOUR

LIVING WITH GREAT EXPECTATIONS

Be not angry that you cannot make others as you wish them to be, since you cannot make yourself as you wish to be.

THOMAS Á KEMPIS

Never sacrifice the permanent on the altar of the immediate.

BOB KRAYNING

When we candidated at our church," said a pastor's wife from Wisconsin, "I passed out cards and asked people to write what they expected of me. The answers were so diverse: inviting members into our home, chairing the women's group, writing a column for the newsletter, teaching Sunday school, singing in the choir, directing the Christmas pageant. Some others said, 'We expect you only to concentrate on your family so your husband is free to minister to the church.' "

She concluded, "I thought if I tried to please the Lord I'd please the church. But it doesn't always work that way."

Children of pastors also feel expectations. One of the most common is the need to be everyone's friend but nobody's *best* friend. The pastor of a rural church in Kansas explained that he'd recently had to have a talk with his 8-year-old daughter, Shandra. She had a special friendship with her classmate Melissa, but another girl her age in the church felt left out. The other girl's parents complained to the pastor that Shandra was ignoring their daughter.

"Shandra wasn't consciously ignoring the other girl," said the pastor. "She simply felt closer to Melissa, and they did things together. But I talked with Shandra and explained the importance of making everyone in Sunday school feel welcome. She's conscious that part of our role in the church is to help befriend everyone."

The Odd Assortment

The surveys and interviews identified some of the commonly felt expectations — some legitimate, some difficult, some impossible:

"They expect our family to be an example. This is legitimate and not a problem except when this means there are two sets of standards: one for the pastor's family and one for everyone else."

"My 3-year-old is 'the church kid,' with an abundance of spiritual aunts and uncles. Of course being a celebrity can be both an advantage and a disadvantage. With everyone feeling like they know her, they expect her to be friendly and give everyone a hug. Sometimes after church she's tired, and people still try to get her to say something cute."

"Our daughters weren't wild about being expected to bail out teachers or youth leaders stumped by theological questions. More than once they found an adult turning their way to ask, 'What do you think? Why did God send Abraham to Israel instead of India?' "

"They expect to see parents fully in control of their children."

"They expect our family to be fully involved in the church and fully involved in the community. They expect my wife to be very active as a teacher, worker, etc. Because my wife works a full-time job, this isn't always possible."

"They expect me to be at meetings I really don't need to attend. One Christmas we were expected to attend eight Christmas parties of different groups in the church."

"They expect my wife and kids to be at every church function. We hear about it if my wife doesn't attend one of the 'women's meetings' or if my daughter opts out of the youth social."

"They expect us to have the answers and to meet their needs. It's hard for them to see us in the battle also. They think we've graduated!"

"They expect our children to attend Christian schools."

"They expect us to always be available — seven days a week, twenty-four hours a day — to put their needs first, and to work for low pay."

"I'm not aware of special expectations for the family, but they expect 100 percent availability from the pastor, and toleration of their demands from the family. They don't understand that the pastor has a legitimate obligation to spend time with family away from church activities."

One female pastor wrote: "My spouse and I used to go away for two days, one week out of each month. I got flak for this from one woman, who told me, 'You're only supposed to have one day off per week. You're gypping the church out of twelve days a year!' "

When I asked one pastor's wife if her congregation had special expectations for her and her family, she said thoughtfully, "I don't know if the problem is expectations so much as lack of appreciation. Whatever my children do or I do, it's seen as what we *should* be doing rather than an expression of commitment and service to the church just like any other family. Somehow people think it's easy for me to teach Sunday school, host the youth group, lead the ladies' Bible study, and plan bridal showers — while everyone else can beg off as 'too busy.' "

It isn't only adults who put pressure on the pastor's family. The kids' peers are sometimes just as guilty. Remembers one pastor: "One of our daughters used to complain that the president of the youth group would never begin the meeting until she was there, even though she wasn't an officer. So even though she was usually on time, attention was called to the times when she was late. She resented this, because anyone else could slip in unnoticed. I'm sure the leader was not trying to embarrass her. He just felt more comfortable when she was there to help the discussion. But my explaining that to her didn't make her feel any better. Young people as well as adults tend to think that ministers' kids should behave better, take more responsibility, and be, if not more spiritual, at least more knowledgeable about spiritual matters than other children."

Sources of the Irritation

Expectations come from a variety of sources: people's preferences, their understanding of Scripture, their previous experience with pastors' families.

Usually the problem is not that any one person thinks the pastor's family should do too much — it's that there are so many *different* ideas of what they should do and be.

"I find very few individuals with unrealistic expectations — it's the composite image that gets to you," says Mike Halcomb, who pastored in Milwaukee before assuming a denominational post. "And rarely does anyone outside the pastoral family see the composite."

Sometimes the expectations of two different people are mutually exclusive, such as when some church members expect the pastor's teenagers to be leaders, role models, and comfortable in the spotlight — and others don't want them getting any special considerations.

Other times the demands, while not mutually exclusive, may pull in different directions. Jim Conway describes the strain this put on him and his family:

"Our first church after seminary was in a small town where a number of our families were farmers. I decided we needed to be up and going when the farmers started their day. At least I wanted the light on in my study before dawn. But the church also had businessmen who worked into the evening hours. So it was necessary, I felt, to please them by serving late at night with various business meetings, speaking engagements, and visitation appointments.

"One day our preschool daughter said to Sally, 'I hate the church, because it takes my daddy away from me.' When I heard that, it was like being stabbed. I was sacrificing my family to make the church happy with me."

Pastors and their families cannot simply dismiss expectations, refuse to be what the congregation desires, and live as they please. If they do, they quickly develop an adversarial role, becoming oversensitive to violations of their rights, which often leads to an arrogant, independent spirit that hurts their ability to minister.

Expectations are part of any relationship. "My three sons have expectations of how we spend money, how we behave, and where we take vacations," said Mike Halcomb. "All these have to be sorted, negotiated, and discussed. And that's the way it is in the church family, too. Ministry involves creative redefining and redirecting of expectations."

"It's a fine line," says Pastor Stuart Briscoe, "and requires open communication about what may be impossible demands."

How do pastors and their families go about walking that fine line?

Handling Expectations

It helps to admit that certain expectations are legitimate. Congregations naturally will expect the minister's family to fit into church life. It's also normal for church members to watch the pastor's family as an example of Christian parents' trying their best to raise a Christian family. And many ministry families are happy to accept these expectations.

"We need to let our congregation know we're a normal family with normal struggles but that we're learning to work through these trouble areas," said a pastor's wife. "If a pastor's family cannot give assurance that they find hope and answers in Scripture, how can they minister?"

One pastor put it this way: "Congregations need to know, and want to know, that the pastor's family isn't trouble free. But they also need to know it isn't troublesome." Between those two poles is where we must come to terms with expectations.

It also helps to recognize that expectations aren't all bad; some are even beneficial. Joseph Stowell reflects on the shaping influence they were on him: "I think being a PK, being in the public eye, helped forge my life. What grated against me at the time actually became a part of my training. Learning to live with people watching you, learning to show deference to people, living with people who expect more of you than they would of others—I appreciate that now."

For him, those expectations were a plus, something to live up to. "It was training time," said Stowell, "because the rest of my life I was going to live in this fish bowl. When I graduated from seminary, I asked my father what I should do — be an assistant pastor? He said, 'No. Go right into the pastorate. You've grown up in a pastor's home. Go for it.' Growing up in a pastor's home is a seminary education in itself. You develop a sixth sense for the issues of ministry."

Pastor's wife Bonnie Halcomb discovered that the expectations of the congregation helped her to grow. "Occasionally people make requests of me — public speaking, for instance — and I'll think, *There's no way! That just isn't me.* And yet I pray about it, decide to give it a try, and many times discover that not through my strength but the Lord's, I am able to. It is a growing experience (and gives me even more appreciation for my husband). Sometimes expectations push us, making us grow in ways we wouldn't otherwise. You can't just automatically say no. Maybe God is opening a door."

Other expectations may be legitimate, but only a minor consideration — the way the pastor and his family dress, for example. Said one pastor: "Our society is more forgiving now than it was years ago about clothing. But I'm still sensitive, especially when someone takes me to meet business associates or to a community group. Initial impressions are important. I don't want my dress to *detract* from what I'm trying to do.

"But I hope we've gotten past the point where smoking a pipe makes you a theologian, growing a beard makes you a counselor, or wearing pinstripes makes you authoritative. Expectations about dress are legitimate but not very substantive."

Still other expectations, however, may not be legitimate or beneficial, and the best way to handle some of these is with laughter. "We always laugh when we think of the time we announced we would be adopting our first son," said Bonnie Halcomb. "One little old lady came to my husband and said, 'That's how every pastor and his wife should have children.' She thought pastors should be sexless!"

Expectations become dangerous when they push a family to live a lie. One mother explained, "You want to please the congregation, and since you think they expect your children to perform in a certain way, you put pressure on them to do so, often without realizing it."

As another mother put it, "There have been times when the kids had the feeling we were more concerned about our image than we were about them."

Blending Expectation and Acceptance

Parents have discovered a key in helping children live effectively in the church environment is blending high expectations with unconditional acceptance. Both are important. If children sense only the high expectations without the acceptance, they feel alone, beaten down. If they receive only acceptance, even for subpar behavior, they can grow up unchallenged and spoiled.

Donald Miller, who grew up in a pastor's home and went on to become pastor of a Christian and Missionary Alliance Church in Missouri, says, "As I was growing up, I was aware

I was a 'PK,' and often the reason was that other folks reminded me of it. If I did something that the older generation didn't agree with, they were quick to say, 'Now we would expect that from other children but not from the preacher's children.' I didn't get that kind of admonition at home. We were just kids like everyone else. There were standards in our home that other homes didn't have, but it was explained to us that it was because ours was a Christian home, not a preacher's home."

At times even preachers' kids will argue, "But the Smith's are Christians, and they let their kids see R-rated videos at birthday parties."

In the face of that kind of pressure, Miller's parents didn't relent, but neither did they hide behind the pastoral image.

"Rather than being reminded that I was a 'PK,' I was reminded of the importance of our name ('we are *Millers!*'). I was urged to live in such a way as not to bring shame to the name and thus to the family. So at home we were treated like the growing children we were."

How do parents show acceptance even in the midst of expectations? One practical way is making sure the children know their parents are easily accessible — even when church work is heavy.

"My kids always stop by the church on their way home from school," says an Iowa pastor. "I'd rather be interrupted during my office work and hear about their day than to make them feel Dad was off limits. They don't stay long, but it seems to be important for them to be able to walk in on their own."

Another way is to know your children's individual personality traits and to adjust the expectations accordingly.

Hank and Mary Simon, who minister in a Lutheran church near St. Louis, have two girls, Christy and Angela.

"Christy is extremely left-brained," says Mary. "She's very organized, almost perfectionistic, and places very high expectations on herself. She's the one who will come home from school, automatically get out her books, and do not only her homework but extra credit and tomorrow's lesson, too. We don't push her because she puts so many demands on herself. Christy is socially tentative when meeting new people.

"Angela, on the other hand, is right-brained. She doesn't worry about details. After a spelling test, for instance, she may say, 'I've got the right letters in there; they're just a little mixed up. What's the big deal?' But she's very intuitive and good with people. It's no big deal for her to go up to people at church and give them a hug. But we'd never ask Christy to do that."

Identifying and accepting the particular traits of family members is the essential first step in determining legitimate expectations to help them stretch.

Adjusting Expectations

At times, we learn to live with expectations. At other times, however, it's necessary to adjust the attitudes of the congregation.

One pastor's wife gives a concrete example of one situation most ministry families face:

"A constant interruption in our lives is the telephone. Besides the normal calls that any woman receives, the pastor's wife must take a large number of calls for her husband. If he is not at the church, people call the house for him. If he is not here (which is usually the case), the caller often asks his question of me. Likely as not I have no idea what the problem is about, but I have to listen anyway.

"There also seem to be a number of people in every congregation who *always* call the parsonage first when looking for the pastor. In spite of the fact that his study is at church, they seem to have the idea that he spends his time hanging around the house. When they are told that he's at the church, they act surprised. And the next time they call the house again.

"I have been late for appointments on many occasions because of phone calls at the last minute. I often think I should take the phone off the hook while I am preparing to leave, and quickly put it back before I go out the door. But I never do."

One pastor's wife, realizing her housework and other obligations were suffering, began to keep track of the time spent on calls for her husband. In one two-week period she spent an average of three hours a day listening to people who really wanted to talk to her husband.

What can be done about this kind of expectation? Can you adjust it? Of those we surveyed, 58 percent of the pastors (and 42 percent of the spouses) said they had tried to change congregational expectations for their families. How did they do it?

1. *Brief the congregation.* Many pastors tell the congregation they expect their family to be treated like any other family in the church — no more and no less than any other church members. This message, most often, is communicated to the search committee and the church board before accepting a call, although some pastors communicate the message even more widely.

One pastor told the entire congregation: "My biggest fear and greatest challenge is to minister well both to my family and to you in the church body. I don't want to be forced into a situation where I must choose between the welfare of my kids and the well-being of my ministry. But I want to state publicly that if that ever were the case, I would choose for my kids. You might call it a 'previous commitment.' I want you to know that now.

"And secondly, I want you to know that we're human. And that means there will be times when my kids are going to embarrass me. You can count on it. And my kids want me also to say there will be times when my behavior will embarrass *them*. I think that's what they call a well-balanced family."

This pastor has found the light-hearted reminder has been well-received and helps defuse some of the over blown expectations.

Donald Bubna, who pastors a Christian and Missionary Alliance church in British Columbia, has also been very direct with the congregations he has pastored. He reinforces his message almost annually. "My wife was raised in a parsonage, usually right next door to the church. Because of her somewhat negative experiences with that, we determined that we would be frequent in extending hospitality, but that our home would be *our home*, a refuge, not an extension of the church, not a place for church business. Therefore, it was not a place for phone calls unless they were of a social nature or an emergency.

"So every year at the annual meeting, after I make my report, I make a statement of appreciation for the people's love for our family. And I'll say something like, 'And I want you to feel free to call me at home any time there's an emergency and you need me. But if it's not an emergency, please call me at the office during regular hours.' I put it very positively. And in the last fifteen years of ministry, I've averaged perhaps one phone call a night. It hasn't been a problem."

Bubna also took steps, while his children were growing up, to neutralize the expectations on them.

"At elders' meetings, from time to time, I'd thank the board members for accepting our children as they were and not putting pressure on them to be different from their own children. But I'd go on to say, 'Your acceptance means so much, and so does the fact that you believe in them. You believe our children will not ultimately fail, and therefore they won't.' I tried to create a climate that balanced acceptance and positive expectation. And they responded well to that."

2. Demonstrate your values. Mike Halcomb says, "I was criticized for announcing a service of house blessing soon after we bought our home. It was with Bonnie's consent, but some women in the church thought I'd done it behind her back because we had the service before we'd cleaned thoroughly, and the house needed some fixing up.

"But we wanted to communicate something. First, our home is an extension of our ministry, a place of ministry. Second, if we wait until everything is in apple-pie order before inviting others over, we'd probably never practice hospitality. We wanted to dash right away any expectation that our home would be picture perfect. We'd rather model something else — hospitality amid the clutter of living — perhaps giving people freedom to use their own homes as places of ministry."

3. *If necessary, politely but firmly make your concerns known to key people.* One Kansas pastor's wife says, "Our daughter was always the one expected to do the prayers or devotions for church meetings and even 4-H clubs. She said she wished they'd let someone else be the 'priestess.' I eventually talked with the leaders and asked if they could pass the responsibility around. Fortunately, they were very understanding."

4. *Don't live for the church alone.* Most pastors periodically remind themselves, yes, God is the head of the church, but the church is not God. He is the only one worthy of our souls.

One way to keep aware of the difference between God's interests and the congregation's is deliberately to develop hobbies and friendships outside the local church.

"We have found other professionals, such as doctors and business people as well as pastors and laity from other churches, to be good stimulators for us. They remind us of what God is doing in the larger world," said one pastor.

Others find that joining a computer club, a community organization, the PTA, or Little League not only helps keep this perspective, but also builds significant ties to the wider community.

5. *Focus on what's truly important.* It's easy to be distracted by expectations. In his book *The Little House on the Freeway*, Tim Kimmel, who ministers in Arizona, has a highly personal approach to keeping perspective:

"In my desperation to remember my priorities, I have set six individually framed pictures across the upper shelf of my rolltop desk at work. The picture on the left is of the Jameson Memorial Hospital in New Castle, Pennsylvania. That's where I was born. The picture on the right is of a six-foot-high granite monument that stands in the middle of the Graceland Cemetery just outside this same town. You can't miss the word KIMMEL carved on its side. The earth beneath it conceals the remains of several generations of my family. The four pictures that sit between these two outer pictures are of Darcy (my wife), Karis, Cody, and Shiloh (my children).

"What we do for a living has a way of absorbing our attention. Its demands are so great and its ego satisfaction so intoxicating that it can easily become the focus of our lives. I love my work, but I don't want it to become the heart of my existence — my reason for living. That's why I have those pictures strategically placed on my desk. When I look up from my studies, I come eye level with a reminder of my purpose. Stealing a peek at them several times a day has a way of keeping my work (and my life) in proper perspective. In the brief moment it takes me to scan them I receive a message in the cluttered back rooms of my brain.

"The pictures say, 'Don't forget, Tim, *this* is where you checked in (the hospital), *this* is where you're checking out (the cemetery), and *these four people* in the middle *are why you are here.' "

All in all, expectations benefit us when they cause us to examine our priorities, when they sensitize us to our faults, and when they bump us out of personal ruts. They harm us if they keep us from being true to the Lord or to our calling.

FIVE

BALANCING CHURCH AND FAMILY

Your family is not apart from your ministry; it's a part of your ministry.

HOWARD HENDRICKS

A generation ago, a man wrote in his Bible, "Let my heart be broken with the things that break the heart of God." That rule ordered his life.

For twenty years, he scurried from Korea to Africa to China to India to Europe saving souls, housing orphans, and building hospitals. Through his documentary films, radio broadcasts, and personal appearances, he awakened the social consciousness of an entire generation of American Christians. In the process, he formed a worldwide relief organization, World Vision, that continues to be one of the most effective Christian relief agencies. The man's name was Bob Pierce.

But while Bob Pierce was reaching the world, he had greater difficulty embracing those closest to him. He accepted the axiom, "If I take care of God's business, God will take care of my family." His consuming work kept him away from home for months at a time. Relational distance increased as time with his family decreased.

He grew sullen, even hostile, toward his family and in time was legally separated from his wife. One child committed suicide; another married prematurely and was soon divorced.

Soon even his closest associates found it impossible to work with him; they removed him from the organization he had begun. He became bitter and reclusive, suffering bouts of severe depression.

Only on his deathbed did he manage one shining evening of reconciliation with his alienated wife and family. He died at peace, but his family life, in many ways, was still in pieces.

The story of Bob Pierce haunts many of us who are committed to wholehearted service for Christ. Must family be sacrificed to accomplish something great for God?

In the corporate world, many would say greatness does come at just such a price. In Tom Peters and Nancy Austin's book *A Passion for Excellence*, they write, "We are frequently asked if it is possible to 'have it all' — a full and satisfying personal life and a full and satisfying, hard-working professional one. Our answer is: No. The price of excellence is time, energy, attention, focus, at the very same time that energy, attention, focus could have gone toward enjoying your daughter's soccer game. Excellence is a high-cost item."

Or consider what David Ogilvy observed in *Confessions of an Advertising Man:* "If you prefer to spend all your spare time growing roses or playing with your children, I like you better, but do not complain that you're not being promoted fast enough."

Granted, Christian accomplishment is measured by a different gauge than the corporate ladder. We'd all acknowledge, even in ministry, that we need to put time, energy, and concentration into our effort. But the story of Bob Pierce has forced many of us to ask the tough questions: Is God honored by a life of tremendous public achievement but private disarray? Does God really call Bob Pierce — or call you and me — to build temple after temple while the foundation of our own families, also a gift from God, crumbles around our feet?

None of us is willing to say so. And yet, the temptation to sacrifice family for ministry, to put other people before spouse and children, continues. Why?

"In many cases it is a genuine love for people and a desire to meet their needs," says Richard Strauss, "but I wonder if other motives don't also cloud the issue. Sometimes we feel a great need for affirmation, but our families see us as we are and don't always give it. Since we can be a hero to a struggling person over there, we spend the time where we get the most praise."

Some clergy admit that their work is their escape. "I was using my ministry to avoid my family," confesses one minister. "When my children got on my nerves, I would say, 'Well, I've got to make some calls,' which was true — there are always calls to make — but I wasn't being fair to my family."

"A lot of ministry is fun — getting up in front of people, teaching them how to live their lives," confesses another. "At times it's a lot more fun than being home changing diapers. And if you've got an excuse to get out seven nights a week, I mean, what wife can argue with God? But that's unfair."

Perhaps because of the sad experiences of people like Bob Pierce, perhaps recognizing the basic unfairness of neglecting family to attend to ministry, the trend in more recent days seems to be going the other direction. More and more pastors are refocusing on the family.

In some cases, this can be healthy. As one minister put it: "I continually have to remind myself I am not indispensable, not personally responsible for the salvation of the world. I *am* responsible for touching the lives around me — especially my family."

This approach, however, can be taken too far. Currently, the most sacrosanct reason for refusing church responsibilities is that "it would take away time that I need to give to my family." Say that, and who can argue? End of conversation. The danger is that we can become selfishly myopic, turning our hearts toward home but our backs to the needs of the world.

A few years ago, Ben Patterson made a highly unpopular observation in LEADERSHIP: "More than once the command to go into all the world and make disciples has put a strain on family life. So has the call to be hospitable to strangers, visit the sick, feed the hungry, and clothe the naked. But today,

Christians can avoid the problematic areas of discipleship in the name of sustaining family life. It is increasingly easy to justify extravagant expenditures on vacations, recreational vehicles, and home improvements because it 'helps build the family.' The truth of the matter is that the family has become a convenient excuse for turning our backs on other people. We want to be left alone to cultivate our own little patch of ground."

Patterson has a point. But so do those who want to avoid the sad example of Bob Pierce. The challenge is to be faithful to both our family and our calling. The question becomes, "How?"

The Delicate Balance

Not long ago I was talking with a pastor who has helped bring renewal to his church and whose family seems to be healthy and strong. By outward appearances, he is doing both extremely well. But when I asked about how he balanced family and ministry, his answer surprised me.

"At any given point in my life," he said, "I can feel good about my ministry or I can feel good about my involvement with my family, but I'm never able to feel good about them both at the same time."

It's a rare moment when we feel totally on top of both church and family responsibilities. Add the responsibility for personal spiritual growth into the mix, and it's even rarer to feel everything is where it ought to be. We all know the surest way to induce guilt is to ask someone, "How's your prayer life?" Ninety-nine percent of the answers will be "Not what it ought to be" or "I wish I could do more."

An Episcopal rector from Washington, D.C., says, "In church ministry and family life, there's always more to do than you possibly can. But that comes with the territory. That's true of any person of vision and energy and drive. Lots of professional people are charged with tasks bigger than themselves. You have to learn to live with a certain lack of satisfaction."

But learning to live with that sense of being continually behind doesn't eliminate the problem. There are still decisions to be made about how we spend our time. How do we decide where we will concentrate our efforts?

Priorities Aren't the Problem

Virtually every Christian today would say that the priorities in life are "God first, family second, and career third." Some, I realize, would take issue with that order. One pastor wrote, "If family is second only to God, what does that say to the full third of our population that is single? God's supreme will for us is holiness, not marriage and family. There is nothing distinctly Christian about a strong family. Buddhists have them, secular humanists have them, and, I presume, even the Mafia has them."

I won't take time to debate fully those issues. I'll assume, based on the fact you're reading a book on the family, that you give it high priority. For our purposes, let's assume the "God first, family second, career third" list is legitimate. The problem is figuring out how to base our lives on our priorities. What does it *mean* to say God is first? How, specifically, do we put him first?

Perhaps you, like I, have heard people say, "The two surest gauges of your priorities are your calendar and your checkbook." Does that mean we should spend more hours alone with God than we spend with family members? Or are we serving God by doing "God's work"? If so, then is church work the way we put God first? Or is church work our "career," a lower priority? The question of priorities easily slides into sophistry.

In addition, the pastor is responsible for two families: the church family and his natural family. Both are given by God. Both are means of serving God. As one pastor wrote: "The

New Testament order is to see family life flowing out of the life of the church. The church doesn't need the family; the family needs the church. The family must be planted in the soil of a vital Christian community if it is to bear the fruit it was meant to bear." Thus, to work for the health of the family, we must work for the health of the church.

Perhaps the greatest problem with the "God first, family second, career third" perspective is that real-life situations can't be quite so neatly arranged. Responsibilities simply don't line up first-second-third. At different times, God, family, and career must each be given our full attention. The issue becomes: When does God deserve my full attention? When does my family deserve my full attention? When does the church deserve my full attention? In practice, priorities can't be stacked like blocks.

To put it another way, we can't watch three shows — no matter how good — at once. So constantly we're forced to ask, *Which channel do I turn to? And for how long?*

How much time should I spend alone with God? Too little time and I shrivel spiritually. But too much time alone can be an escape from other God-given responsibilities.

Likewise, too much time with family can be seen as laziness. One associate pastor repeatedly showed up late to the office and took extra days off without the board's permission. His reason: "It's important to me to spend time with my family." The board members agreed wholeheartedly; they decided to relieve him of his responsibilities (and salary) so he could find another position more in line with his priorities.

On a lighter note, a recent *New Yorker* cartoon shows a woman hanging up the phone, her children standing around with horrified expressions. She's saying, "Bad news, kids. Dad just quit his job to spend more time with the family." Even family members aren't always sure just how much they want Dad around.

And, yes, too much time can be spent on church work. "There's nothing more intoxicating than the adrenaline released by running a smooth operation," says Wayne Jacobsen of The Savior's Community in Visalia, California. "I've been in a position where eight decisions demanded my immediate attention, with two phone calls holding and a counseling appointment in the lobby. It's exhilarating, and the appreciation expressed by many people for our efforts is part of the brew — but the rush of personal importance has nothing to do with the affirmation of the Spirit." No, serving the church is not necessarily serving God.

God, family, career — each is important. None can be neglected.

I asked one pastor how he balanced family time with church work, and he said, "With difficulty! Whichever one I'm concentrating on, my conscience tells me I should be spending more time on the other."

Right now, I'm away from my family writing this book about family life, an irony that hasn't been lost on me, nor on my wife, Susan. You, in turn, are reading this chapter, and in so doing, you are not at this moment involved in deep and meaningful interaction with your family. And yet, I'm convinced (and I trust you are, too) that this exercise is worth the investment. Both my family and yours will be strengthened because of the time we've put into this book.

The point of all this? Simply that it's difficult to define when we're serving God, when we're serving the family, and when we're serving our career. That's true of pipefitters who work for the glory of God and the sustenance of their families; it's even more true of pastors who work in the church.

The issue is not simply getting priorities in the right order; it's fitting them together and finding room for them all. And that challenge never ends — even for a family specialist like James Dobson. "I must admit that the problem of balancing career, church, and family is a constant struggle," he says. "It is rarely possible to realign priorities once and for all. An imbalance can occur in a matter of days. The moment I relax and congratulate myself for having practiced what I preach, I tend to say yes a few times when I should have said no — and suddenly I'm overworked again."

Instead of seeing God, church, and family as competing demands, I find it helpful to imagine church and family as the two seats of a teeter-totter, and God as the fulcrum underneath. We aren't expected to sit in both seats simultaneously (though we may find ourselves, like daring kids, standing somewhere in the middle with a foot on each side of the balance point). The amount of weight we need to place on either side is determined by our God-measured priorities. Where we place our energies at a particular time will vary, depending on where we're needed most.

But all our efforts, whether with the church or our families, are undergirded by the Lord. He is the pivot point for both family life and church life.

Whether we're concentrating on the church or focusing on the family, our task is to make the most of our efforts. There are a number of helps for maximizing our efforts in ministry. (One of them, of course, is LEADERSHIP, a journal I'm a bit partial toward.) But I've not found many resources directed at pastors who want to maximize their efforts with their families. So let's turn our attention to that concern.

WINNING THE WAR FOR FAMILY TIME

God, who is liberal in all his other gifts, shows us, by the wise economy of his providence, how circumspect we ought to be in the management of our time, for he never gives us two moments together.

FRANÇOIS FENELON

Time is what we want most, but what, alas, we use worst.

WILLIAM PENN

Ministers who want to make the most of their family time immediately bump into a complication: the skills required for being a loving parent and spouse — cheerful leadership, attentive listening, nourishing words, caring — are the same ones demanded by the pastorate. This can be an advantage if the nurturing skills developed in ministry can be applied to the family.

But it can be a decided disadvantage if the "people helper" finds his people-helping capacity given over to the church family during the day and depleted by the time he leaves the office. The family gets whatever happens to be left over.

Keith Meyer, who pastors in Maple Grove, Minnesota, said, "One day, half an hour after I'd walked in the door, my son came up to me and said, 'Are you home yet, Dad?' He knew it took me a while to reenter the family after a day at the church."

Other pastors know the feeling of "not being all there" even when they're there. No one is happy with a half-attentive zombie. Are there ways to improve the quality of our time with our families?

Strategies for Quality Control

The first strategy is to be sure that at the end of the day you bring something home: a healthy attitude. That can begin before you ever leave the church.

One pastor in Canada makes sure to work off some of his tension before he gets home. "Sitting at my desk all day is a sure way to guarantee I'll be edgy when I come home," he said. "So now I make sure I take a brisk walk sometime during the day. Even if I have a full day, I find that one of my conferences can become a walking conversation, and we'll walk for an hour. That's a great tension reliever."

To remind herself that her day isn't over when she leaves the church, the director of children's ministries at a church in South Dakota has jotted a quote from Socrates (apparently the temptations in 450 B.C. weren't too different from today): "If I could get to the highest place in Athens, I would lift up my voice and say, 'What say ye, fellow citizens, that ye turn every stone to scrape wealth together, and take so little care of your children to whom ye must one day relinquish all.' " She's reminded that the pursuit of wealth — whether material goods or spiritual treasure — is vain if we overlook our heirs.

A second strategy is to make a definite mental switch on the way home. Or, if that's not possible, do something once you arrive that signals to yourself and your family that you're home at last.

"We have a standing joke in our house: Dad isn't home until his tie comes off," says a minister in Indiana. "I usually shower, shave, and change my clothes when I get home. It refreshes me and helps me make the transition to family life."

It's hard to make that mental switch. Reliving the day is natural, but we can spend so much time thinking about the church and what we can do to improve its quality of life that there's not enough think-time left for the people closest to us. And even though we may be preoccupied with church problems, or simply fatigued, our mental vacancy is interpreted by our family as disinterest. Maybe we *are* disinterested — after listening to people all day, it can be hard to be attentive to a 4-year-old's chatter. Those times call for heroic action: putting aside lofty thoughts of ministry (and putting down the newspaper) to make eye contact and enjoy a few minutes of touching and talking with the *other* important people in our lives.

A third strategy is to let the family know you've been thinking about them in your absence. For some, this means recounting conversations during the day in which you were able to say a good word about some family member. Or perhaps it's something you give them when you arrive — an interesting story from the day's activity, or something more tangible.

A minister recalls, "When I was in seminary, my children were preschoolers. I stopped at the library every day on my way home and checked out one children's book to read to them. They knew I was thinking about them while I was away, and I was compelled to sit down with them as soon as I came home." This minister adds, "My temptation is to put my family on hold — at least until they 'snatch me back,' sometimes vigorously. But if I am too busy for my family right now, I will be too busy for them ten years from now. And they will learn that being too busy for one's family is acceptable, for I will have taught them that lesson myself."

A fourth strategy is to remember the family deserves at least the same care any other parishioner would get. Being away from the church doesn't mean all responsibilities are over. When Gordon MacDonald was pastoring in Lexington, Massachusetts, he learned this the hard way: "It used to be my habit to 'be comfortable' on Monday mornings and come to the breakfast table unshaved, unwashed, and generally undressed. One day my wife asked me, 'Why are you so carefully dressed and groomed for God and the congregation on Sunday?'

"I said, 'I want to offer them my best.'

" 'Then what are you saying to the family by the way you dress — or don't dress — on Monday?' she asked. Pow! She had me. From then on, whenever we're together as a couple or as a family, I'm careful to be as sharp and alert as possible in my mental attitude, dress, and common courtesies. Whatever I would offer to church members, I want to offer that and more, if possible, to my own family."

A fifth strategy is to control the telephone, that invader of family privacy. While it's not possible or desirable to eliminate people's access to you via the phone, some pastoral families have found it beneficial to limit it at certain times.

"At times we turn the phone off when we're home at night so we're not prisoners in our own house."

"We take the phone off the hook during supper or moments of family discussion or periods when study or meditation are extremely necessary. In twenty years I can hardly recall a moment when being instantly accessible was necessary. We have learned not to let the phone become our master."

A sixth strategy is to include the family in certain aspects of the ministry. A number of pastoral families mentioned that some of their best times were participating in ministry together — church socials, camps, even visitation.

"Last December, a single parent in our congregation who was struggling financially was *given* a Christmas by an anonymous donor," said one pastor. "I was asked to deliver the food and gifts. I took the kids along, and they still talk about the thrill of seeing the joy and gratitude of that mother and her girls."

These strategies are possible avenues to quality time together.

Quality time, though important, is not sufficient. A certain quantity of time is prerequisite for quality. In the business world, if a company wants a better product, you don't hear supervisors saying, "Don't worry about how much time you put in as long as it's quality time." No, when it's time to produce, most companies expect overtime.

And in relationships, too, amounts are important. As David Seamands once observed, "A young lover wouldn't get by telling his fiancée, 'Honey, it's not the quantity; it's the quality. You have my undivided attention for the fifteen minutes a week I give you.' She wouldn't fall for it, and our families don't, either."

What are some ways pastors ensure they give sufficient quantities of time to allow quality time to emerge?

Strategies for Quantity Control

Here's how some pastors approach the quantity question.

Long-range plans. One of the false hopes of family life is that because next month's calendar is currently fairly open, next month will actually be less hectic than this month. It's tempting to say, "Things should lighten up if we can just get through the next two weeks."

Unfortunately, by the time you get through the next two weeks, the two weeks after that have filled up, and you find yourself looking hopefully at the two weeks after *that.* It's a deadly plague known as "creeping calendar commitments."

This condition has driven many pastoral families to plan family times at least a month ahead.

"Six to eight weeks in advance, we write in major blocks of various sorts of private time," says one pastor. "We get these on the calendar before the events of church life begin to appear."

"Since I believe my family *is* the Lord's work just as much as the church, I write my family members into my Day-Timer as I would for anyone else from the church," adds Kent Hughes of College Church in Wheaton, Illinois.

How much family time realistically can be scheduled? This varies depending on family and church situations, but several pastors use the following rules of thumb:

• One night a week completely free of anything but family activities — a time for the family to be together.

• One night a month alone with spouse — either an overnight getaway or at least a leisurely dinner date.

• One event a month alone with each child — perhaps an outing to the zoo or a museum, or even something as simple as breakfast at McDonald's.

Other families develop their own rhythms, but most affirm the value of planning the times they'll be together. If left to "whenever the calendar is blank," somehow those times mysteriously disappear.

One of the benefits of this kind of planning is enjoying the anticipation of special events. "We always try to have our next family vacation scheduled and written onto the calendar," says one pastor's wife. "In the words of Scripture, this gives us 'a future and a hope.' "

The weekly routine. There was a lot of variety in the survey responses on the question, *How do you balance family time with time spent on church work?* Some typical entries:

"I try to be home on Monday and Friday evenings, for all meals, and to see the kids before they go to school in the mornings."

"I'm always home from 5:30 to 7:00 P.M. to share the meal with my family. Then I'm almost always home two of the five weekday evenings and on Saturday afternoon and evening. Once a week we go out to eat in a nearby city."

"We have a rule of thumb for our congregation that we try to have no more than three nights a week for church events. And I try to model that for the rest of the congregation. So everything has to fit into Sunday night, Wednesday night, and one other night. That means we usually do some hospitality on Sunday night after the evening service. Wednesday is spent at church, and any committee meetings are the third night out. Of course, any social commitments would be a fourth night, but they don't count as church business."

While some pastors try to limit the nights of church activities, others work from the other direction; they schedule family time first. One pastor gets the family together once a week at breakfast to plan when they're going to be together that week.

An Episcopal rector draws on his English roots for family time: "My wife and I have struggled throughout our marriage to have enough time to talk and pray about things that are important. We tried to have a date night, but between her schedule and mine, finding one regular night of the week was virtually impossible. So we've taken to 'tea time' late in the afternoon but before supper."

Another key strategy is the use of the day or day and a half off to which most pastors are entitled.

Maximizing the Day Off

Virtually every pastor gets a day off — at least is *supposed* to take a day off. This is the church's concession to "balancing" time at home and time at church. How do pastors go about making the most of that time when that's all they have for personal rest, errands, household chores, and family time?

One question on which pastors differ is which day of the week to take off. Many take Monday, either because that's the day they're most tired or because that's the day decreed by the church. Others, however, say that's *not* the day to take because the natural letdown after Sunday means they're not giving their families a day when they have normal energy. "If I'm going to be mildly depressive, I'm going to do it on company time," joked one pastor who does paperwork and administration on Mondays.

Many others take Saturday off because that's the day their kids are off from school. But that's not satisfactory for some because so many weddings fall on Saturday, and even when nothing is scheduled, they find themselves preoccupied with the next day's sermon and activities.

Others take another weekday off and try to take advantage of school holidays. One pastor reports taking occasional family outings even on school days. "Sometimes we'll take the kids out of school for a special family excursion. Last week we took Monday off and went to see a special display at the museum. You can't let school stand in the way of an education," he says with a grin. Nor in the way of a memorable family event.

Veteran pastor Donald Bubna, while at Salem Alliance Church in Oregon, had a policy that staff members would work 5½ days a week. "We recommended they work six days one week, and then take two days in a block the next week. They had to take them that month — they couldn't be carried forward." That approach allowed for more rest and the opportunity for two-day getaways.

Wise use of the day off is one of the easiest ways to acquire a quantity of time sufficient for quality moments. But another element of family life also deserves attention.

Vacations

I once asked a panel of PKS who grew up to be pastors, "Did you ever resent the demands ministry placed on your parents? Were there times you felt other people had stolen your parents' attention?" They all admitted the time pressures and the many evenings parents were away, but resentment? As one panelist put it, "No, but only for one reason. Vacations saved it for me. If we hadn't taken our vacation as a family every year, I would have felt resentful, I think.

"My dad didn't make a conscious effort to do something with me five days a week. He had meetings; he was gone a lot of evenings. But two things stand out in my memory that demonstrate to me that Dad did care for me and that I was important to him.

"Several times he took me to Yankee Stadium for the Memorial Day double header. Or on an occasional day off, when he didn't go to the office, I'd say, 'Dad, let's go see the Yankees.' And he'd take me.

"Then we also took the whole month of August for vacation, and we drove to Michigan, where my grandparents lived. And Dad and I would go fishing on the St. Joe River. We had a rowboat, and we'd row up the river and fly fish as we drifted down.

"I think those times saved me. For eleven months he belonged to other people, but in those ways, he said, 'You are important to me.' "

Many pastors have found vacations an important time to build family unity. On the other hand, a vacation doesn't necessarily mean restful togetherness. Doug Self, who pastors in Redstone, Colorado, describes an all-too-common occurrence:

Last summer we planned a family camping trip. My wife and I had visions of relaxing in the hammock, sitting romantically around the campfire, taking nature hikes with the children. Unbeknownst to us, the children were thinking, *Let's be entertained. Mom and dad will be doing neat stuff with us.* We were on a collision course. I'd just stretched out in the warm sun, ready to devour an old copy of *Reader's Digest*, when the first squabble broke out. Then a child's voice moaned, "I'm bored; there's nothing to do here." Strange, I thought I'd just exploded that myth by my reasoned explanation. You know what happened next. When children are bored, they get into bickering with each other: "I had it first." "No, it's mine!"

Somehow children don't seem sensitive to parental feelings or able to adjust their behavior accordingly. This bothers me as a dad. Sometimes, being a pastor, it bothers me even more. I sometimes feel I am regarded as an "emotional rock" by people in my congregation. I listen to problem after problem and help when I can. People, presuming my strength, say things that hurt. So when I come home, I'm sometimes looking for emotional support, understanding, and pampering. My wife is having problems of her own, drained by her daily round with the kids and house. I walk in the door to demands and complaints. "Hey, wait a minute," I want to shout. "I don't need this. Pastors and dads sometimes need to be cared for, too." But it doesn't often happen. Certainly not on vacations. It's just a fact of life that again must be accepted and endured.

What are the keys to a good vacation? The favorite places to go and things to see will depend upon the family, but pastors have found some principles important in making vacations a building time for the family.

1. *Remember that "working vacation" is a contradiction in terms.* Yes, many pastors take families to conferences and speaking appointments, and these can be enjoyable for the family, but they're not always the best time together.

"I have three weeks of vacation, and I decided a few years ago not to take *any* work with me," says a Colorado Springs pastor. "On earlier vacations, I always felt vaguely guilty that I wasn't getting to the books I'd brought along. I wasn't really on vacation at all. Now I take no work along. I even tell the church, 'Please don't call me. Well, if the church burns down — maybe. Just get my books and illustration file out, *then* you can give me a call.' "

2. *Learn to enjoy strategic recreation.* "I've learned to match my recreational pursuits with family needs," one minister explains. "I saw early in my ministry that I could not pursue a recreational life with friends and still have time to pursue a *second* recreational life with my children. Therefore I chose early in life to do things for recreation that my children could join me in doing: canoeing, camping, hiking, and other activities where our exercise and togetherness could be maximized.

"I fear too many fathers spend time on tennis courts, golf courses, and in health spas and then wonder why they never have prime time with their children. I'll admit, though, this has been an easy doctrine for me to embrace since I'm a terrible tennis player and I've never broken a hundred in golf, even for nine holes."

3. *Learn to enjoy the time you do have.* Pastor's wife Dreama Plybon Love tells about her rude awakening to the demands of ministry. She and her husband decided to get back early and spend their last day of vacation relaxing at home.

"It sounded like such a good idea — sleep late, enjoy breakfast out, go for a leisurely walk," she wrote in *Partnership* magazine. "We were in bed asleep, having returned home at 4 A.M., when the doorbell woke us. My husband put on his robe and stumbled to the door. A member of our church was waiting. He looked quite somber.

" 'Sorry to bother you, but yesterday my wife had surgery for breast cancer. She would like to see you at the hospital.'

"At first I felt genuine compassion, but gradually concern turned to resentment at the intrusion. Couldn't we have this one day just for ourselves? Our vacation had been hectic, crowded with friends and family. We needed this time together. Was I being selfish, even cruel, to want to extend our vacation in light of this man's need?"

She and her husband had been married only six months at the time, and already she was struggling with the questions: *Must we always make choices between marriage and ministry? Can I not love my husband and serve my God at the same time?*

What eventually happened on that cherished and curtailed vacation day?

"It wasn't so bad. We stopped at the florist and made a hospital call; but we were still able to take that long, leisurely walk. As we walked we planned *next* year's vacation, and I think next time we'll give ourselves a full week alone — before we come back home."

Freedom to Choose

Do the demands of ministry force us to overactivity? Not according to one pastor, who reminds us of our ability to determine what path we will choose.

"I've heard so many times, 'Because of the demands of ministry, I neglected my family,' as if they were somehow compelled to. For solo pastors and senior pastors especially, I found that an invalid excuse. Ultimately we decide how much we're going to give. The challenge is to fulfill both ministry and family roles, but we have the freedom to find creative ways to do that. Perhaps we'll have to be out every night some weeks. But we can often grab lunch or spend even a full morning with our spouse. We may have to cut out something else, but we have that freedom."

At times, however, this freedom has to be asserted with emotional resolve. William Tully, rector of St. Columba's Episcopal Church in Washington, D.C., described one such painful incident in an article that appeared in the *Washington Post*:

Most afternoons I break off work and meet my sons' school bus. This is my key family obligation, since I end up working most evenings and at least half of every weekend. (My wife's job downtown doesn't allow her the afternoon flexibility.)

One recent afternoon, while my son, Jonah, 8, took part in an afternoon choir rehearsal, his 12-year-old brother, Adam, and I found time for a long-postponed (by me) game of catch. I had impressed him — and assuaged my guilt — by having ball gloves all ready to go. Just as we got into our game on the church lawn, a regular parish visitor — a down-and-out street alcoholic — showed up and wanted a handout. Many times before and since, St. Columba's has helped this man. But since the other clergy who assist me were away that day and the secretaries in no position to help him, he stood on the sidewalk and demanded I pay attention to him.

"I'm not working now. Can't you see?"

The booze in him made him belligerent. "What kind of priest are you, man? You won't even listen to my story."

I ran up for a pop fly that Adam had expertly launched.

"That's right. Besides I've heard it before. I'm sorry, you'll have to try somewhere else or come back another time."

He turned to go back to the parish office and unleashed a string of obscenities.

"Get out," I shouted. "If you ever want my help again, you'll just have to move on."

It was then I realized that several passersby, probably fresh off the Metro at Tenleytown, had stopped to watch. A few choir mothers had come to the church steps to behold their rector having a tantrum.

I still haven't sorted out the rush of conflicting feelings I experienced then. I did feel strongly that my family came before my vocation. I was also composing fantasy headlines in my head: BUSY NORTHWEST D.C. PRIEST FORGETS SAMARITAN, SHUNS POOR MAN. I imagined parishioners listening skeptically when words like *charity* and *sacrifice* pop up in sermons. Still I shagged my last pop fly that day knowing that ethical choices are always messy, that my strong suit is not social justice, and that the words I treasured most that day were, "Thanks, Dad. Great game."

CHILDREN AND CHURCH LIFE

Children of the ministry are not volunteers; they are conscripts.

DOUG TOUSSAINT

My job as a parent is a temporary responsibility with eternal consequences.

TIM KIMMEL

What do Alice Cooper and Cotton Mather have in common? Not much, except that both grew up as sons of ministers.

The same is true of Aaron Burr, Orville and Wilbur Wright, Walter Mondale, John Tower, Marvin Gay, Martin Luther King, Jr., and Sir Laurence Olivier. Other "preacher's kids" include Albert Schweitzer, Christian Barnaard, and Harriet Beecher Stowe.

There's no guarantee, of course, that *any* child — whether born into the home of a preacher, professor, plumber, or prince — will decide to live in a way that brings honor to God and joy to parents. Nor can pastoral couples guarantee even that their children will find church a place to enjoy rather than endure. Some factors are beyond parental control — critics, conflict — but parents can help prepare children for church life, interpret what's happening, and create an atmosphere that makes church life much more appealing and increases the chances of the child's developing a strong relationship with God.

Let's look at some of the key elements in helping kids have a healthy experience in their church life. Family-conscious ministers have identified several general strategies.

Fathering or Pastoring Your Family?

The first is to recognize the difference between being a father to your family and being your family's pastor.

When your family is part of your congregation, you'll wind up pastoring them. As one Nazarene pastor pointed out about his children, "I'm the only pastor they've ever had." Through preaching, counsel, and example, pastors provide spiritual direction for everyone in their congregations, including their families.

But there's danger when a pastor sees his family only as objects of pastoral care and not as intimates with whom he has a qualitatively different relationship from the one he has with ordinary members of the congregation.

"I may pastor my family, but I don't want always to be their preacher," says a pastor from San Diego. "I struggle with dads who preach at their kids but don't listen, who have an agenda for every conversation: Dad speaks, kids listen. I have a tendency to be like that. But I'm grateful that God gave me a wife who won't let me. I don't want to be the family preacher, except on Sunday."

A pastor from Michigan says, "I don't think of myself as my family's pastor. I do pastor them on Sundays. But when I walk in the door at night, I don't think of them in congregational terms. My home is my escape, a place where I don't have to be The Pastor."

In some ways, fathering is a much easier role, a more natural fit, one that doesn't require us to maintain the poise and energy level of pastoring. But in other ways, it's a more uncomfortable role.

"I can stand up in front of hundreds of people on Sunday and articulate a spiritual principle and illustrate it. People even take notes. But that afternoon, sitting with my wife and kids, it's a lot harder. No notebooks come out!" says Joseph Stowell with a smile. "I'm not nearly as articulate or convincing. I've given talks to teenagers on dating, morality, and handling temptations. I tried to sit down and cover that with my kids. It didn't work. I wondered, *What's wrong with me? I just lost the gift.* That's the difference between fathering and pastoring. Fathering is a very different role — our impact goes beyond the realm of precept. Our impact comes from our character, attitude, integrity — our caring and love for them."

One way to make sure the preacher/authority role is occasionally shucked for the "just plain ol' Dad" role is to capitalize on situations where we are *not* in charge. A minister living in New Hampshire illustrates: "My son plays soccer, and I enjoy games as a spectator. But I've turned down all invitations to coach or even be an assistant. Why? Because whenever Mark enters my world, he always sees me in charge. I want soccer to be one area where he is in charge, where he knows more than I do, and where *he knows* he knows more than I do. All I do is show an interest, ask questions, and learn from him."

Orienting Children to the Ministry

Orientation is important in helping children handle the realities of life in a ministry home. If they are prepared, they aren't as likely to be jolted by difficult people or situations.

Most pastors and spouses surveyed indicated they brief their children to expect people not to be perfect. But they also try to help them see the importance of ministry.

"I try to teach them that the church is not above hurts, criticism, and conflict. These are growing areas — great teaching times," writes one pastor. "As a family, we endure the bad, enjoy the good, and grow in both. We're teaching them to be liberal in gratitude, and to write notes of thanks and praise to encourage others. I often speak of the faithfulness of God's people through the ages."

"We pray as a family for hurting members," writes another.

Yet another pastor is not quite so delicate in his choice of words: "The number one issue for me has been to let them know I love the Lord and the church he died for — and because sheep are sheep, there's frequently lots of sheep dung to clean up. So we're not shocked when sinners sin."

Each of these expresses in a different way the same truth: children of ministry benefit from periodically being briefed on what to expect.

Entering Each Other's World

Parenting books stress the importance of spending time with your children. And who would argue? But many of these books leave the impression that parents should eliminate the important and interesting activities they enjoy and bore themselves silly with coloring books and Parcheesi.

While it probably wouldn't harm any of us to join our preschoolers with the Play-Doh or our junior highers with the video games, involvement doesn't always have to mean descending to the level of a child in order to relate.

Preacher's kid Tim Stafford describes his own upbringing: "My father didn't join the neighborhood football games; we probably would have been embarrassed if he had. He never played Monopoly with us. He encouraged us in our chosen vocation of fishing, but he never bought a rod and reel himself. I always had the impression that we were kids, allowed the kiddish dignity of going about our kiddish affairs in all seriousness, without adult interference.

"I am not certain I can recommend my father's lack of involvement in our interests, but I strongly recommend his alternative — involving us in his. He allowed us to enter his world when we were interested in doing so. He and I trekked hundreds of miles in the back country of the Sierra Nevada together, not so much (I believe) because he was being a good father but because he wanted to go. We talked baseball because he was avidly interested. He also liked taking us to meetings with him. I remember particularly one Sunday night when after the evening service, I went with my father to a hotel restaurant to join a small circle of pastors chatting with Addison Leitch, one of my father's most admired seminary professors. I didn't know what they were talking about, but to this day my memory can bring back the rich pleasure of being allowed in adult male company as a sort of equal."

In some ways, the elder Stafford was showing his son the same respect he'd show for any friend — he sought common ground. Hopefully, one of those mutual interests will be ministry. This was the situation for another pastor's son, who grew up to become a pastor himself: "I was raised in a parsonage, and my dad was never there. Most nights it seemed he had some meeting to attend. But I never resented it because he included me in his life."

One way to begin doing this is, as some church leaders do, to grant kids an open-door policy.

Bill Bright, the founder and president of Campus Crusade for Christ, says that when his children were small they always had access to him. No matter what important visitor might be in his office, the boys were always allowed in for at least a brief greeting. Dr. Bright wanted them to know that their concerns took precedence over any other problems he might be dealing with. He did not want them to feel they had to make an appointment to see their father.

Developing a Ministry Mindset

Most pastors would love to have family members share their commitment to ministry. How can that commitment be encouraged?

One key is to teach children to do what we are trying to do — live for God's glory and not our own. This results in their becoming what sociologist David Riesman calls "innerdirected." They learn to act on the basis of the strength God gives, to do what they know is right, instead of bowing to pressure from their peers (or even their parents).

A pastor's wife from Indiana offered the following example from when her daughter was in third grade. "One of her classmates had parents who both worked during the day, and he would come home to an empty house. One day he started playing with a cigarette lighter, and the house caught fire and burned to the ground. After that, everyone at school made fun of him and called him 'Lightning Bug' or 'Firefly.' When he would take his lunch to a table to eat, the others would get up and move away. Our daughter told me about it; she was quite upset. She explained that he was not a special friend of hers — she didn't even like him very much — but she was concerned about the way he was being treated.

"I asked, 'What do you think Jesus would want you to do about it?' She thought a minute and said she thought Jesus would want her to take her lunch and go sit with him. I agreed. So the next day at lunch she sat next to him, taking her little sister along for moral support. The following day a couple of others joined them. By the end of the week he was integrated into the group again. This was an amazing incident for me to observe. A basically timid child had found the power to resist peer pressure to help someone in trouble."

By pointing the child to God, this approach can help avoid a contest of wills between parents and child, because the parents aren't saying, "This is what we want you to do." They aren't even saying, "The Bible says." They are helping the child to develop his conscience and to make decisions on the basis of his growing knowledge of God and faith in him. This, of course, is much different from using "God's will" to pressure children into bowing to "parents' will."

One minister's 12-year-old daughter, who had been raised with a ministry mindset, was able to use her sanctified social skills to help some of her friends at a party. During the games the popular boys were continually choosing her and her pretty friends for partners. The hostess, who was not pretty or socially skilled, was being neglected. The minister's daughter was sensitive to this and cornered two of the most attractive boys. She told them they had a responsibility to pay attention to the hostess. After all, they had accepted her hospitality. "We can take care of ourselves," she said. "You go pay attention to her." And they did.

These, then, are some general strategies for helping children have a healthy church experience. Now let's turn to specific situations.

When the Children Are Young

Pastors have several techniques when their children are preschoolers or in the early elementary grades.

Bedtime briefings. Even preschoolers can benefit from briefings, if they're handled simply and with imagination.

One church leader says that bedtime has proved the best time for this with his daughters. He explains: "Saturday night, or any night before a church event, as I'm tucking the girls in, I tell them about the good things to expect the next day — the friends they're going to see, the things they're going to do. And I'll try to tell them what to be listening for; I give them a foretaste of any lesson or sermon they'll be hearing. If I know the Sunday school lesson, for instance, I'll tell the Bible story. My girls like that because (1) they feel more confident the next day when they hear the story, and (2) I throw in more detail than their teachers usually do. Our daughters especially like to know names for each of the characters.

"Once, for instance, my 3-year-old's teacher was telling the story of Jesus' healing the blind man. Stacey was eager to tell the class, 'His name was Bartimaeus!' a detail the teacher had somehow managed to overlook. Right now, our daughter is troubled because she knows the names of Noah's sons — Ham, Shem, and Japheth — but I can't tell her the names of the sons' wives who were on the ark, and her inquiring mind wants to know! But I'm glad to supply her with little details. I like to fire her imagination for the next day's activity."

Church as second home. Because they're at the church so often, children will naturally begin to see it as their second home. A number of pastors have tried to use this fact to their advantage.

"As our children were growing up, we tried to let them see the privileges that go along with the pastorate," said Kent Hughes. "For example, they got the run of the church building during the week — gymnasium and all."

Jamie Buckingham, now pastoring in Florida, said that when his kids were small, "we wanted them to feel the church was an extension of their house, so they were welcome in the office — and occasionally during worship one of them would come up on the platform and stand with me during the congregational singing. I allowed that because it didn't disrupt our worship, and it helped reinforce that the church was *their* place, too."

Warm associations. Many pastors try to make sure their kids associate church with positive feelings. Part of this comes naturally through friends, caring teachers, and the positive perspective of parents. But at least one pastor did even more.

"I've always sat on the front row with my family during worship services, not up on the platform," wrote this pastor. "I go to the pulpit only when I have a specific task to perform. Otherwise I've always been sitting there stroking my children's hair, scratching the back of their necks, kneading their shoulders — and they never wiggled a muscle for fear I would stop. We never had a behavior problem in church with either of them. Now that they're older, they simply would not miss a church service — and I've pondered whether their faithfulness is not built to some extent on a subconscious association with good feelings of warmth and intimacy."

Avoiding after-service neglect. The period right after the worship service is an important time for the pastor to make contact with people. But a crowded narthex can be a confusing place for young children, especially when both parents are concentrating on greeting worshipers.

One pastor's daughter told about trying to talk to her father in the foyer after the Sunday morning service. She shouted, "Dad, Dad," but she couldn't get his attention. Finally she said, "Pastor!" and got his immediate attention. Understandably, she felt her father was more interested in others than in her.

"I know that my children will superimpose the image of their father, to some degree, upon their understanding of God," says David Goodman, pastor of Winnetka (Illinois) Bible Church. "Most kids do. I don't want my kids seeing God as one who is interested only in others and not in them. At the same time, the time in the foyer after a Sunday service is crucial ministry time."

So he has devised an arrangement. "We get someone, usually one of the single women, to get our two youngest kids from their classrooms and watch them for the forty-five minutes right after church while we're busy. We pay her, and sometimes she takes them to the park across the street, or, if the weather is bad, she plays with them in a room in the church.

"We don't need child care for our 10-year-old; she's seeing her friends and talking to other people. (I think one of the advantages for kids growing up in a church home is that they tend to be well socialized; they get more interaction with adults.) But for the two younger ones, we had to get child care because otherwise they get into mischief. After all, they've been in church two to three hours already, and if we're too harsh on them, they begin to resent the whole experience. That's the last thing we want. We want them to enjoy going to church as we enjoy going to church."

When Children Are Older

In the later elementary-school years and beyond, strategies change. Here are some methods used by ministry parents who have preteens and adolescents.

The first and most common is to *involve the children in various aspects of the ministry*. One way is to pay them for office work. "I'll often bring one of my kids to the church when he or she needs to earn a little money," said John Yates of The Falls Church in northern Virginia. "There's always some filing or sweeping that needs to be done, and I pay them out of my pocket.

"My dad was in the department store business when I was young. I started working there when I was 12, and he'd pay me out of his pocket. It made me feel special that my dad was in charge of this organization, and that I could work there, too. And the employees loved Dad's children. Well, I see that same kind of feeling among the children here. This is a happy church, and my kids feel loved when they come here to work."

Another way to involve children is to take them along on certain kinds of visitation. Hank Simon of Signal Hill Lutheran Church near St. Louis, Missouri, takes his 10-year-old along every time he visits Mrs. Keller, a long-time member of the church who is a shut-in. And over the years Christy has grown very close to "her shut-in." Mrs. Keller often has little treats for Christy. For instance, when Christy took her an Easter basket, Mrs. Keller had some chocolate-covered peanuts for her.

"Christy is learning that caring is part of the Christian life," says Mary Simon, Christy's mom. "Now she's worried because the woman's cat is more than 14 years old. Recently she asked me, 'What will Mrs. Keller do when her cat dies?' I was touched that a 10-year-old could care so deeply for her elderly friend."

Another time, Mary Simon remembers, Christy stood on the footrest of a wheelchair so one of the blind people could feel her face. Finally the woman said, "Thank you. I'm so glad to see you."

"Our daughters remember visiting the 101-year-old lady in the nursing home — and going to a funeral of a young child," said Mary. "By being involved in ministry this way, they have developed a good sense of life's stages."

John Yates took his 11-year-old son to a dinner where John was to be the speaker. "They invited my wife and me, but Susan was busy that night, so I asked if I could bring my son. The hosts agreed. Well, you might think he would have been bored stiff at a formal dinner with a bunch of old people. But he wasn't. Afterward he said, 'Dad, that was a great talk.' And he even enjoyed talking with some of the people. Later one of the older ladies wrote him a letter and sent him a gift — a Bible. It turned out to be a great experience for both of us."

Yet another strategy is *occasionally to single out children for special treatment*. A number of pastors' kids recall their parents doing something especially for them, even amid the busyness of ministry. This event often made a profound and lasting mark on their attitudes toward ministry.

Richard Strauss remembers: "When I was about 5, my dad had a portrait taken of just him and me with our arms around each other, and he wrote across that portrait, *Pals.* He hung it in his study. I used to go in when he wasn't there and just stand and look at that picture. It meant more to me at that age than anything in life. In fact, I've got it at home now."

At times, pastors' kids seem to need an occasional reminder that they're "more special" than the members of the congregation. One of the best reminders: periodically spending time one-on-one. Sometimes this requires firm resolve. One pastor, who was also the son of a pastor, recalled a key moment in his upbringing.

"In addition to pastoring, my dad worked a second job, 3–11 P.M. five nights a week, to support our family. But about once every other month, he would do something one-on-one with each of us kids. One Saturday morning, it was my turn, and Dad and I were getting ready to go hunting."

Suddenly a car pulled in front of the house. It was Wilbur Enburg, one of the elders, and he wanted the pastor to come with him.

"It's Joe and Laura," Wilbur said. "They're upset and say they're going to leave the church. I think you should go see them."

"I talked with Joe last week, and with Laura the week before that," the pastor said. "The situation can wait."

Wilbur wasn't happy. "I think you should see them today."

"Sorry," said the pastor as his son watched silently. "I'm going hunting today."

Wilbur's face got red. "If you go hunting, don't bother to come back." Then he turned to get back into his car.

"I don't think you mean that, Wilbur," the pastor said. "I'll see you in church tomorrow."

The pastor's son reflects, "As Dad and I headed off to the woods, I had to ask, 'Is this going to cost you your job?' "

" 'I don't think so,' Dad said. 'But if it does, the job is not worth keeping.' "

Sure enough, the matter with Joe and Laura was not an emergency. They did not leave the church, and the pastor's ministry remained intact. And the pastor's son learned a lasting lesson: his dad considered him more important than pleasing a particular elder. That affirmation has lasted nearly forty years.

This story, however, raises another question in giving children a healthy church experience: How to handle the conflicts and difficult people that arise in any church? How do these affect the children?

The Critical and the Contentious

When difficulties arise in church life, parents face the challenge of explaining to the kids what's happening without souring the children's attitudes toward the church. The approaches will differ depending on the ages and maturity levels of the children, of course, but some of the key principles remain constant.

Most pastoral families try to shield their children, especially in their younger years, from exposure to the criticisms and conflicts of church life.

"We don't want to poison their attitudes toward the church or toward any individual," said one minister's spouse. "So we don't roast the congregation at the dinner table. We try to focus on the positive things happening in the church."

Of course, there will be times when children will eavesdrop on conversations, or, when a critic phones you at home, they'll overhear your side of the conversation. They may sense your discomfort or hear you desperately trying to phrase an appropriate response. Then, after you've hung up the phone, what do you say?

"After I've been discussing a church problem on the phone," said a California pastor, "often our young children will ask me, 'Who was that on the phone?' I'll say, 'Someone from church,' and if they press for details, I'll simply tell them, 'It's not your conversation.' "

As children get older, however, and begin answering the phone themselves, they'll know who the other person is, and when they sense from your responses that there is tension, a bit more explanation may be in order.

Most pastors let their children know that other people often see things differently — and that's okay. They don't bad-mouth the people but try to explain the differing points of view.

One tough situation is explaining why a particular family is leaving the church.

"I'll try to give people the benefit of the doubt — 'they felt they had legitimate reasons, and people need to find a church where they feel comfortable,' " said one pastor on the survey.

The most important principle seems to be: Don't overstate the seriousness of the conflict. If you're going to err, err on the side of *under*stating the problem. Children don't have the perspective their parents do. They have a hard time under-standing that "5 percent of the congregation is giving us a hard time." Instead, their lasting impression is likely to be "the whole church gave us a raw deal" — an attitude that can have long-lasting effects.

One pastor tells of a mistake in handling church tensions: "A man has been harassing me recently. He wants me to do something I can't do. Our board has discussed the issue, and their decision has been clear. But this man feels I should override the board's decision. He and I have discussed the situation many times; he has called me at all hours — even 4 o'clock in the morning! I had to hang up on him a time or two.

"The other night my 11-year-old daughter answered the phone and told my wife that Mr. Smith wanted to talk to me. I was upstairs, but my wife, knowing the situation, said, 'Tell him your Daddy can't talk to him right now.'

"My wife immediately regretted that she hadn't told Mr. Smith herself, because it tore up my daughter. She didn't know the situation, but she knew I was home. She naturally wondered, *Why won't Daddy talk to him?* She sensed the tension, and she was scared. So that night I tried to explain that I'd tried to help the man, but couldn't, and he kept bothering us. When she realized there wasn't a genuine need, she could accept that. But she should never have been put in that position."

Learning from that mistake, the parents now vow to handle such encounters themselves.

Gordon MacDonald, reflecting on his three pastorates in three different states, said: "I don't think the kids ever heard us talk negatively about people. Frequently Gail or I would say, 'This is a tough week for us, kids. Dad's under a lot of pressure.' Or 'Dad's had a few disappointments, so I may not be myself.' But I wouldn't say, 'Joe Brown is really socking it to me this week.'

"Yes, there would be times when they knew somebody had called frequently. So it was not unusual to say, 'You need to know that Mr. and Mrs. Smith are having a rough time these days. Mom and Dad are helping them. You may see them here at the house for a while tomorrow night. We'd really appreciate it if you'd just breathe a prayer for Mom and Dad that we can find the best way to help.' As the kids grew older, they would join us in praying for these people and would delight when we would bring them good news about so-and-so. We didn't break confidences. But we did paint broadstroke pictures for them so they understood the things they observed."

Another pastor, F. Dean Lueking of Grace Lutheran Church in River Forest, Illinois, established specific ground rules for talking about church conflicts.

"I always try to operate by this principle when I'm with my children: to talk about adversaries in such a way that if they were present, they'd feel their views had been fairly represented. I often find myself saying, 'I can see why he feels that way, even though it distresses me.' "

This practice gives children a healthy perspective on conflict. They see that even while people differ, respect can be maintained.

At times, though, Lueking found he needed to invoke a second ground rule, "our four-minute rule."

"Especially at the dinner table," he says, "we would put a limit of four minutes on conversation about congregational troubles. Then it would be on to the Cubs, vacation plans, our reading, or whatever. Pastors can go on and on about church problems, and I wanted to make sure that didn't dominate our talk and our thoughts."

Dealing with the Curious

Sometimes parishioners treat the pastor's kids as sources of inside information. One pastor reported the following encounter:

Ed Bailey, a middle-aged parishioner, approached the pastor's 10-year-old son in the narthex after a morning service.

"Hi, Josh. How's school?"

"All right," said the pastor's son.

"That's good. Say, you know Marilyn Mason, don't you?"

Josh nodded. Marilyn was a single woman who sang in the choir and occasionally helped in his Sunday school class.

"Has she ever come over to your house?"

Josh didn't know what to say. He knew Marilyn had come over to talk to his dad and mom, but he didn't know about what. So he said, "I think so."

"How many times has she been there? A lot? Did you see her there this week?"

"I don't know," said Josh. Finally Ed quit the inquisition. Josh felt uncomfortable, and at home that afternoon he told his dad what had happened.

The pastor was irritated. "Marilyn had been coming to my wife and me for encouragement and counsel about some family concerns. Ed was a friend of Marilyn's older brother. I told my son that the situation was none of Ed's business and that I was sorry he had been put under that pressure." He let his son know that he had done the right thing in pleading ignorance. "I told him it wasn't his fault and assured him that I would handle the situation. I wanted to take all the burden for this off my son."

So later that week, after he had calmed down, the pastor called Ed. "I told him that Josh had mentioned the conversation and felt uncomfortable because he didn't know what to say. I asked Ed please not to put my children on the spot. I suggested that if he needed information, he should get it from me."

Ed was silent. He didn't offer an explanation for his curiosity, nor did the pastor ask for one. But the calm confrontation was effective.

"That was two years ago," says the pastor, "and Ed didn't seem offended. More important, he hasn't grilled my kids since."

How do you prepare children to respond to nosy members of the congregation?

Some ministry families tell their children only what they would be willing to share with the whole church. This is reasonably effective with younger children, but as they get older they will naturally observe the seamier side of ministry — frayed nerves, differences of opinion, criticism, conflict. Some children develop a sixth sense for what is appropriate to talk about with church members; other children may need some guidance.

One pastor instructs his children simply to say "I don't know" or "You should ask Dad about that" when people ask for information about specific people.

Another ministry couple teaches their children that certain things are talked about only within the family. "When our kids were young, we distinguished between 'good words' (which they could use anytime) and 'bad words' (which they were *never* to use) and 'secret words' (mostly bodily parts or functions, which we were to talk about only within our own family). They've been pretty good about honoring our understanding about secret words. As they're getting older, we're able to build on that concept to explain that other kinds of things also stay within the family."

Another pastor put it this way: "We'll tell our children what other people in the congregation are likely to know. We want them to hear the story from us rather than from anyone else, if possible. So with sensitive information about someone, I've often said, 'Here's what other people know, but let's not be the ones to talk about it, okay? That's gossip.' Our kids respond well to that. We let them know we're trusting them, and we want to continue to develop that attitude of trust."

Capitalizing on the Compensations

Perhaps the most important element in helping children have a good experience in the church is not to prepare them for the bad times but to accentuate the good experiences.

"I remember how rude people at church seemed to be to us kids," says Chuck Smith, Jr. "After a service, I'd be standing there holding Dad's hand, and they would step right between Dad and me — coming between us both literally and figuratively. They either ignored me or seemed annoyed that I was there, since their lives were falling apart and they had to talk to the pastor. I grew up hating adults, these people I always had to be polite to.

"But Dad was sensitive to what I was feeling. He would let me hang on to him, grab his pant leg, and I never heard him say, 'Go away. I'm trying to talk to this person right now.' "

In addition, Chuck remembers his father's going out of his way to make sure his son also realized the *benefits* of being the preacher's kid. "He had a saying — 'When your dad owns the candy store, you're treated to certain privileges.' For instance, one time Dad was the director of a week-long summer camp. He took me along, and most of the time I was kind of lonely because he wasn't really there for me. There was always a crowd of people around him. I caught him only coming and going.

"But one evening, everyone was finishing dinner, and he came to my table and whispered, 'Grab your swimsuit and meet me at the pool.'

"The pool was closed then. But he opened the lock and we got in. I'll never forget it — just Dad and me swimming in the pool. It was like he 'owned the candy store' that weekend. As camp director, he had access to the pool, and he wasn't breaking any rules by going in there with his son. Things like that were very special to me."

THE MINISTRY OF MARRIAGE

The rite of ordination does not override the rite of marriage. Both are noble callings, and one is not the "higher calling." Both were instituted by God for the sanctification of his people. By some curious act of his grace, this sanctification includes the clergy.

GREGORY P. ELDER

Eventually, every minister's wife runs into some element of church life that makes her life difficult. Sometimes the experience is jarring. Consider the following true story:

"We arrived at our first pastorate at the end of September, having been delayed by an accident on the way in which my tailbone was broken. Since I was nearly eight months pregnant at the time, it did not heal until after the delivery. I had to do my work alternating between periods of standing up and lying down. I carried an inflated rubber ring everywhere I went, since sitting on it helped to ease the pain a bit.

"Somehow, I managed to get some boxes unpacked, and even started toilet training my toddler. The ordination service, at which my husband was to be officially installed as pastor, was set for the end of October. I played the organ for the service while perched on my rubber ring. Afterward I served sandwiches, dessert, and coffee to about thirty people in the parsonage. Everyone seemed to think it was my job, and I never questioned it.

"Our second baby was born on November 14. This released

pressure from my tailbone, so it started healing. I was nursing the baby, and all was going well. The basement still contained boxes needing to be unpacked, many windows were waiting for curtains to be sewn, the toilet training of our toddler had hit an impasse, and I remember brief moments when I doubted that, should I live to be eighty, I would ever get my dishes and ironing all done at once, but all was well. My husband was enjoying his work, and the people were generous. We were showered with everything from eggs and chickens to cookies, honey, and cream.

"Then, about the middle of December, it happened. One of the Sunday school teachers asked me what I was doing about 'the Christmas concert,' referring to the Sunday school program. I had no idea what she meant. I repeated her words back to her, stalling for time: 'The Christmas concert?' Then she explained, as one might to a not-very-bright child, that the minister's wife always took care of the Christmas concert. This meant she produced and directed it and usually wrote the script as well.

"The previous minister's wife was an older woman with no children. She loved to do this sort of thing and had lots of experience. I, on the other hand, was a very young, very busy mother of two babies, one only a few weeks old, and I had never even taught a Sunday school class.

"The incredible part of this episode is that I did it. I really did, on two weeks' notice, throw together some sort of a program. I still remember standing up there directing with perspiration streaming down my face. Immediately afterward I went home, nursed the baby, and collapsed in bed.

"They never should have asked, I never should have even considered the request, and my husband should not have allowed me to accept. But at that time none of us knew any better."

An extreme case, perhaps, but this type of experience is not uncommon. Not many years ago, the accepted model of the minister's wife was that of an active partner in ministry, and this was accompanied by certain expectations about how she would dress and tend the home, and what she would and wouldn't do in congregational life. One wife said, "If I do too much, I'm 'running things.' If I'm quiet and reserved, I'm 'not doing my share and fulfilling my role as the pastor's wife.' "

Though most pastors' wives I contacted said that changing times were easing some of the traditional expectations, some irritating assumptions remain. For instance, when the church can't find anyone else for a particular job, "of course" the minister's wife will do it, or "we can always get the minister's wife" to give the devotions at the women's gathering.

"It's interesting that I'm the only woman in the church who is never thanked for doing a job," observed one wife. "I like sharing my talents, but it's hard to be taken for granted as if I've been hired to work here."

Most wives find they are expected to fill in for their husbands as a listener and counselor. Many find that having people trust them with personal concerns is gratifying. Others, however, feel uncomfortable and ineffective in this role.

Some pastors' wives take naturally to the challenges of the role. For most, however, there are at least moments when they feel lonely or out of place. According to the LEADERSHIP survey, it may be a greater problem than their pastor/husbands are aware of. When asked, "Has your spouse ever felt lonely or out of place in the congregation?" 68 percent of the pastors said yes. But when we asked the pastors' spouses, "Have you ever felt lonely or out of place in the congregation?" fully 76 percent said yes.

One pastor who did recognize his wife's feelings described the situation this way: "I have the greatest wife in the world, so any victory in ministry is a shared victory. But sadly, for her, the victory is always vicarious. But the loneliness is personal."

The first step in addressing an issue is understanding the factors that contribute to the problem. What factors lead to this sense of loneliness?

Alone in a Church Crowd

Some of the factors can simply be peculiarities of a given church. For instance, sometimes the age of the pastor and spouse inhibits close friendships within the congregation.

"The leaders in our congregation, the people with whom we spend the most time, tend to be older than my wife and me. As a result, we feel a bit left out of relationships with people *our* age," wrote a pastor on the survey. "Plus, we have no social life apart from the church."

Neither are younger pastoral couples immune from the fact that mothers of preschoolers will naturally tend to feel isolated. "My wife's most difficult times were when our children were very small and she was tied to home duties, while I was seldom at home during the day and sometimes not in the early evening," confessed a pastor. "Her complaints struck sympathetic chords in me, but sympathy was not what she wanted!"

Another pastoral couple felt the same problem from the opposite side. "As we got older, the people who were coming onto our staff seemed younger and younger. We were mentors to them, but not exactly friends. We were old enough to be their parents. In the past, we'd been close with others on the pastoral team, but now they find their own web of relationships. And I think my wife feels the loneliness even more than I do."

A more common reality that can increase the loneliness factor is that church members often see pastors and their spouses as different from ordinary folk. Some wives have mentioned that in Bible studies or small groups, people turn to them, expecting answers to troubling questions simply because they are married to a minister. These spouses feel awkward sharing their own honest doubts and unnamed terrors for fear of shaking the faith of younger, more fragile believers. Thus, instead of being a source of relief from loneliness, these groups only reinforce it.

"We pastored in a small town in the Midwest," said one

pastor's wife. "The people were warm and friendly in church, but no one seemed to want to be close friends. I figured maybe they thought pastoral families wouldn't be around long enough to form lasting friendships. But then I met a woman who seemed friendly and tenderhearted. She always asked how I was doing and how I felt about things. She would tell me she missed me if I was not at a service, but she never invited me to her home. After a Wednesday night prayer meeting, I invited her over for tea while our husbands had a meeting. She appeared hesitant, but she came. During the conversation, she told me she couldn't be close friends with the pastor's wife because it might offend other people. I was hurt, to say the least, and it made me hesitant to try to be close to any other woman in the church."

Fortunately, not all churches share that attitude, But in any church, a bright spotlight seems to focus on the clergy marriage. The feeling of being watched can increase the feelings of loneliness.

David and Vera Mace, in their 1980 study of clergy couples, found that 85 percent felt their marriage was expected to be a model of perfection. They wrote, "Clergy couples are almost obsessed with the feeling that they are expected to be superhuman and to provide models for the congregation and community." Another study notes that "Protestants consider their minister's personal and family life as 'tools for ministry.' Unfortunately, family modeling is often measured by moralistic 'thou shalt nots' of public behavior rather than by how families handle deeper issues."

The problem is not so much the high expectations but how the pastoral couple responds to them. If clergy couples are trying to live out other people's expectations of a perfect marriage, it can be hard for them to deal with their own real marriage, which leads to a game of "let's pretend." As one minister said, "Congregations desperately need clergy marriages to work. They think that if their ministers can't make it work, how can *they*? That's an awful burden!" Even more stressful is when the couple knows they are falling short of these expectations, but they don't feel able to ask for help.

Other contributors to loneliness emerge not from the congregation but from the natural tendencies of ministers themselves.

The education and emotional gap. A few years ago, I met Mary LaGrand Bouma, a pastor's wife who has written *Divorce in the Parsonage,* and asked her, "What makes for *meaningful* communication in a ministry marriage?"

She said, "If I had to pick one thing, it would be commensurate education. That may surprise you — I know it certainly did me when I was doing research for a book on pastors' wives. I interviewed two hundred ministry wives, and when I read through my notes, I said, 'I can't believe this.' Healthy marriages in the ministry were those in which the wife's education had *not* been cut short.

"Many wives work hard and long to put their husbands through seminary, and what do they get? A silent husband who assumes she cannot function on the intellectual level at which he has now arrived. I thought I had found an exception to this rule when I interviewed a pastor's wife in Seattle whose marriage I knew was strong. I asked if she had studied beyond high school — and was suddenly embarrassed: she had not even finished high school. But as it turned out, *neither had her husband.* They were part of a group that didn't require seminary or even college, and they had done a lot of informal learning together. As a result, they got along extremely well.

"The marriages in trouble were the marriages with big educational gaps. Why is that? You think differently once you're college trained. That's why I counsel ministry wives to get their college education, even belatedly if necessary."

Another idea: "My husband and I would never have developed our common interest in evangelism if we had not gone to several seminars together. We would discuss the material and new ideas we had heard. After this refreshing time together, we would be inspired again for our ministry. We would set goals together to try some of the new ideas."

The education gap can be narrowed, but often a major chasm, an emotional gap, remains.

David and Helen Seamands point out that this emotional distance often begins during ministerial training. "A communication problem often arises because the man is oriented to books and theology, and shows little interest in the practical things of the home," says Helen. "He is attracted to the ministry because he loves studying the Word and digging into ideas; he conceptualizes everything. The kind of woman most attracted to the life of a minister's wife is a warm, loving, people-person, who sees everything in terms of relationships. When these two get together, they have little common ground for communication."

As a result, the wife can feel starved emotionally, because the husband is unable to express emotions well. "Often, instead of saying what he's really feeling, he preaches at her a principle of marriage from Ephesians 5," says David. "We've found that ministers who come to marriage enrichment retreats are tough to handle because they cannot identify or express feelings. Instead of sharing themselves, they preach."

The secret is to work on staying in touch with one another on both intellectual and emotional levels.

The preoccupied pastor. Ministry demands concentrated energy and attention. Unlike an hour spent chatting about sports, an hour spent counseling a couple considering divorce can leave a minister emotionally exhausted. One pastoral couple described it as the difference between a bucketful of feathers and a bucketful of rocks — the measured amount is the same, but the scales tell a different story.

Many ministers struggle not to lose touch with their spouses in the midst of touching everyone else. If the ministry becomes a "mistress," many times the children can adjust — they may not know any other lifestyle — but the wife is more likely to take it personally. She finds herself losing out to the other love in her husband's life — his work. The irony is that part of the job of a pastor is to encourage marriage. As a pastor's wife put it, "I know my husband is committed to marriage, but I'm not sure he's committed to *me*."

"At the church I'm a man on a mission," confessed a pastor. "But at home my wife is asking, 'But what about me?' " Even church successes can be misinterpreted. "I'm glad the ministry is going well," wrote a pastor's wife. "But when that's the main thing he talks about, I feel that's more important to him than I am."

These factors, then, contribute to the all-too-common feeling among ministry spouses that they don't quite fit. How can those of us in ministry help our spouses have a healthy church experience?

Helping the One Closest to Us

One ministry couple, Dennis and Barbara Rainey, discovered that the key to ministering *to* one another was shoring up one another's self-esteem. Here's how they described it in an article titled "What You See Is NOT All You Get" in the February 1988 issue of *Christian Herald*:

She was as smart as she was pretty. In fact, she was chosen as one of the university's "Top Twenty Freshmen Women."

As a child, this young lady received love and encouragement from her parents — and the example of a stable marriage. There was little stress for her. Life seemed perfect . . . until junior high.

While her other friends reached puberty quickly and began to develop physically, she did not. Her chest remained flat and her legs skinny, and her hips developed no contours. Throughout the first six years of school, she had felt confident, sure of herself, popular. But as she was slow to develop, she began to question her worth. This self-doubt was further fueled by her best friend, who one day asked, "Are you sure you're a girl?"

Those words hit like a lightning bolt from a dark cloud. Fear that she would never develop began to whisper in her inner spirit. Her personality changed. She became quiet, reserved, shy. Comparing herself with others, she always came up short in her own eyes. She felt unpopular, unattractive, awkward, and alone. And no one knew of her fears.

Eventually, she began to blossom. In fact, she became very pretty, yet inwardly she continued to see herself as inferior, and she thought everyone else saw her that way, too.

Determined to forge a new identity, the young woman decided to go to an out-of-state college where she could start fresh. She succeeded. Honor after honor came her way. She pledged one of the top sororities on campus. She earned good grades, participated in numerous campus activities, and became very popular.

Yet no one, not even she, realized that at the heart of her performance was a little girl who was afraid to be known. The accomplishments gave her confidence a boost, but she still needed someone who really knew her to accept her for who she was apart from her achievements.

One year after her college graduation, she fell in love with a young man who appeared to have it all together. He was the extroverted, confident person she was not. Their whirlwind romance found them married after only four months of dating.

She later found out that, although he was secure, he had needs, too. He was impulsive, brash, and overzealous. And behind his air of bravado and pride, he was hiding some insecurities of his own.

After nearly a month of marriage, both began to realize much more was going on inside each other than they had bargained for. One night, after an evening out with some friends, they stayed up talking about how inferior she felt in public settings. Her questions about her worth stunned him. He couldn't believe that this beautiful woman, his wife, could possibly feel that way about herself. He had confidence in her. But her withdrawn behavior at social gatherings began to irritate him. He silently questioned, *Why does she retreat into her protective shell of silence, when I feel so comfortable with people? Why can't she be like me?*

After several of these late evening "chats," he finally realized his wife really did have some serious self-doubt.

That young couple was us more than fifteen years ago. At that time, we had critical choices to make. Would Dennis accept Barbara fully and love her during her periods of self-doubt? And would Dennis be vulnerable and risk being known by a young woman who might reject him? The choices were real. The decisions were tough. In retrospect, we believe those days were among the most crucial in our marriage. In those initial months, the foundations of acceptance and the patterns of response were laid.

As our fears and insecurities surfaced, we also discovered the critical importance of a healthy, positive self-concept to a marriage. We began to recognize the magnitude of the responsibility we each carried in building up or tearing down the other's self-esteem. And we both began to see that our own self-image either crippled or completed our marriage relationship.

This couple learned the importance of building up each other, which not only strengthened their marriage but also benefited their children and those to whom they minister. Because when people see how Dad treats Mom in everyday life, they also, without realizing it, develop an understanding of how Christ relates to us, his church.

What are some specific ways to shore up self-esteem in your spouse? Any good marriage book would suggest: showing warmth and acceptance, sowing positive words, seeing the past in perspective, offering freedom to fail, and so on. But in ministry families, the ministry to a spouse takes on some added dimensions.

Show her you enjoy your time together. You may not have twenty hours a week of private time together, or even ten, but carving out some relaxed, enjoyable time with your spouse is one of the most significant ways of telling her she's important to you.

Robert Crosby, a youth pastor in New York, revealed the dawning of this realization upon him: "Twenty-five youth workers were, for the first time, cooperating to reach thousands of high schoolers for Christ. Definitely the biggest city-wide outreach I had ever worked on was only two weeks away. Over the past six months, I'd spent countless hours of planning, promotion and perspiration. We were about to make history. I was ecstatic. My comrades were thrilled. My wife was disgusted. And I didn't even realize it until I pulled out my personal calendar one day to look at the harried upcoming week only to find Thursday penciled in, PLEASE KEEP THIS DAY OPEN FOR PAM AND KRISTI (my wife and daughter).

"We hadn't had any heated debates or snide comments, but this action cut me to the heart. I had been having so much fun with the youth event that I had been perfunctory in my prior covenant of Christian service — spousing and parenting. Instead of a haven of rest and relationship, my home had digressed into a fast-food restaurant and a place to sleep at night."

How do pastors find enjoyable time with their wives? Here were three of the more unusual ideas I came across:

1. "After the kids are off to school, my wife and I have a long, leisurely breakfast every Friday. We each take our calendar, and we talk about the schedule for the upcoming week and develop our 'to do' list. But we also talk about what's happening in the family and make sure we're looking ahead and asking, 'When are we all going to be together this week, next week, and so on.' "

2. "My wife, Karen, helped me understand that staying away from home 'to do the Lord's work' was oftentimes just veiled selfishness on my part. So we've divided each of our days into trimesters: morning, afternoon, and evening. We've agreed to give outside pursuits (including my church work) eleven segments, and no more than two are allowed

each day. So, if I work in the morning, and I have an evening meeting, I do not work in the afternoon. Unless an emergency arises — and it rarely does — after eleven segments, I'm done for the week. It was difficult, but in time, I worked five days a week. At the same time, Karen enjoyed two sacrosanct segments per week to be away from the children (and me, if she desired)."

3. "Between the kids and church activities, we have virtually no uninterrupted hours in the evenings. At night we're both emotionally exhausted, and I realized if that was the only time we were spending together, that was poor planning. So we look forward to a regular midmorning rendezvous. The kids are off to school, and I'll come home from the church for a couple of hours. It's quality time to get reacquainted emotionally and sexually."

Protect her from the system. At times, "the system" — the expectations of a church — can become overwhelming. One way to build self-esteem is to help confront those unrealistic expectations. Sometimes it's easier for the pastor to say "enough is enough" for his wife than it is for her to do it herself, and this support is a powerful affirmation. Here are a few ways this has been done by pastors surveyed:

"I recognized that I'd encouraged my wife to be involved in church ministries — Sunday school, children's church, etc. — which is good, but in our case it had been overdone. She was missing valuable contact with people our age. She didn't have any fellowship. We worked together to be sure she had a chance for social times."

Another pastor on the survey wrote: "My wife has sometimes felt out of place, usually as a result of unfair criticism or gossip suggesting she does too much or not enough, says too much or not enough, etc. We talk it out, and then, at times, I've stepped in with a *loving* confrontation with the critics over the phone or in person. In most cases, this has resolved the issue — and it's certainly brought my wife and me closer together."

A pastor's wife wrote: "Recently a group in our congregation asked my husband to volunteer me for a certain job that he knew would have been an emotional trauma for me. He told them he wasn't even going to ask me, because he knew it was not something I should be doing. I was grateful he protected me that way. Knowing he'll back me up is a big morale booster."

Encourage her search for friendship. Most pastors recognize they cannot be everything their spouse needs: confidant, companion, counselor, pastor, closest friend. As one wife said, "When my husband is my pastor, I keenly feel the lack of having someone else to turn to in times of personal or spiritual need. If I'm 'spiritually dry,' for instance, or if I'm having difficulties with my husband, I wish I had another pastor to go to."

In addition, because of their position, pastors' spouses may find it harder to talk to a counselor — sometimes because of their own reluctance to admit difficulties, other times because of the attitudes of would-be counselors.

One wife told of being at a large hospital during the time her son was dying. She desperately needed someone to talk to besides her husband. A social worker came to see her, but as soon as she learned this grieving mother was married to a minister, the social worker said, "Then you won't be needing me."

The answer, of course, is to find a friend. For some, this has been someone in the congregation; for others, someone from the community; for still others, another minister's spouse has become a close friend. But for both the spouse *and* the pastor, these friendships have proved a treasured gift. As one pastor wrote, "The greatest help for *me* in dealing with the pressures of ministry was when my wife found some other ministers' spouses who shared her outlook on life and ministry."

To Serve and to Protect

One of the most sensitive issues in the husband-wife relationship is whether or not to have secrets. Are there things that should *not* be shared with a spouse? This is a particularly complex area for ministry couples.

The task of a spouse is to both serve and protect his partner. Serving includes self-disclosure — discussing what's going on, especially things that affect your emotional condition, job performance, or future in the church. On the other hand, pastors must maintain varying degrees of confidentiality, which may preclude telling everything they know. In addition, a number of pastors feel that "to protect" their spouses includes not revealing information that would only cause unhealthy emotional distress.

Here's how some pastors have sorted the times to share and not to share.

What TO share. Michael E. Phillips, who pastors at Lake Windermere Alliance Church in Invermere, British Columbia, discussed in a 1988 LEADERSHIP article some of the things he makes sure to tell his wife: "Almost everything that goes on in my life. From the seedling thoughts of a sermon series to the interesting details of a half dozen home visits, my wife shares my day. She relishes the high points, looks appropriately concerned over the troubled moments, and adds her observations whenever she feels it's proper."

That scenario holds true in most pastors' homes. But to be a bit more specific, Phillips identifies two subjects that he's always prepared to discuss with his wife:

1. Difficult decisions. "Every so often, my wife and I celebrate 'Want Ads Day.' It's an event that is cherished by neither of us but demands dual participation. At regular intervals, the pressure of pastoral responsibilities convinces me there must be a softer wall to beat my head against. Therefore, I tell my wife that we are going to look through the classified ads to see what other job I could pursue. Kathy's role is to convince me I really don't want to do anything else. But she has to be subtle; I feel I'm facing a tough decision.

"At the end of this madness, we fold the paper, and *then* my wife asks me what's getting under my skin. Usually, I'm trying to decide if God is calling me to adjust my ministry, or even to change the location. It's always a difficult decision, so I share it with the one who would be directly affected by it. Life throws up difficult decisions the way a plow digs up rocks. They seem to be always there, always annoying, and always tricky to handle by yourself.

"Several months ago, I became concerned that most of the elders were not attending prayer meeting. I decided to confront the issue at the next board meeting by proposing changes in the format of the prayer time, lecturing the board, and soliciting their attendance on Wednesday nights. With glee, I described my plan to Kathy. Her face soured, and she came right to the point: 'Do you really want a prayer meeting full of guilty, shamed elders? Maybe they all have good reasons for not being there.' She then left the room, leaving me to my decision. I knew instantly that she was right. The beauty of her intimate counsel is that it combined objective integrity with conjugal caring. She knew me and she knew my board. And because she wasn't directly involved, she saw the problem with greater discernment than I did."

2. Points of growth. "In my ministry, I take great pains to be transparently honest, showing the congregation that I'm flesh and blood, failing and burdened. I believe it has been effective in that people accept the Word of God from their sinner-pastor with a belief that if I can live it, so can they. Over the years, I have found it progressively easier to discuss intimate failures and personal points of growth.

"Yet it is so hard to do the same with my wife. She even remarked to me a few years ago that if she wanted to find out what God is teaching me, she would have to pay closer attention to my sermons. I was properly corrected. It's part of human nature to fear pain from our most intimate relationships. But it's part of good mental health to overcome that part of human nature.

"A caution: it's essential to understand our problems prior to laying them out before anyone else. We need to be sure we can describe things accurately before we alarm our loved ones. Can you imagine a company's telling its stockholders every conceivable problem in the firm? The stock would be worth zero, even if the company had very little the matter with it."

Other pastors have added a third category of subjects that should be shared with spouses.

3. Problem resolutions. A pastor in Kansas told this story: "My temptation is to tell my wife about church problems, but when the problem is resolved, I'll forget to tell her how it has worked out. As a result, she can get a picture of the church that's skewed toward the negative.

"I had a problem with our former pastor talking with members of our congregation and second guessing my initiatives. I shared my frustration with my wife, and she joined in my feelings. Later, when I was able to sit with the former pastor and clear the air, I discovered he had *not* been trying to sabotage my ministry; the people in the congregation had misrepresented what he'd said.

"My mistake was in not talking about that with my wife. Oh, sure, I told her I'd patched things up with Mel, but I'd spent hours talking about the frustrations and a minute or so describing the resolution. It wasn't fair to my wife. I notice she's still defensive when we're around Mel. I did her a disservice by poisoning her attitude."

What NOT to Share. Marriage counselors talk about open, honest communication between husbands and wives. But there are dangers in openness, depending upon the spouse's interests and capacity to handle stressful information. As one Canadian pastor said, "God lays upon each person a different yoke. There are aspects of my calling that my wife is not called to bear."

One pastor who responded to the survey was concerned about raising his wife's frustration level with a troubling situation when she couldn't do anything about the situation: "When I return from a difficult meeting, usually I can work through the personalities and pressures that cause people to criticize me, but if I give too detailed an account to my wife, she carries it around for several days, and it affects the way she sees these people. So there are some things, especially conflicts, I don't share with her because I've learned she doesn't take it well."

Other pastors want their spouses to be unbiased toward certain people, so they don't share negative things that might prejudice them. Others want their spouses to be free of intra-church controversies as much as possible. "My wife finds that some people will test her to see how much she knows," says one minister. "They'll say things like, 'It's a shame about MaryLou, isn't it?' And my wife is glad she can honestly say, 'I don't know. What happened?' It allows her to be free, sponta-neous, and affectionate toward people."

Michael Phillips identifies a few other categories of unwise topics of conversation.

1. Others' attacking me. "I once asked my wife to describe the one thing I had told her that was harder to handle than any other. Without hesitation she said, 'The letters you showed me last fall.' The previous autumn, I had received a series of nasty notes from a former member of our congregation. Clothed as prophetic words, they were vindictive slanders and generally throw-away advice. After a while, they were laughable. Without thinking, I showed them to Kathy one night. It took her a long time to go to sleep that evening. All she could think about was the dirt this person had thrown my way.

"She was much more upset than I was. Her protective feelings were creating a whirlwind of emotions, alternating between bitterness and anger. Thus I learned that it's a major mistake for us to unload second-hand attacks on our wives.

"What I do now with a situation like that is simple. If I have to tell someone, I tell my prayer partner. He's a good friend, has broad shoulders, and never gets upset at attacks on me. He thought the letters were funny; he even got me laughing over them. Kathy still doesn't laugh when she sees the letter writer and his wife downtown. She has, however, worked her facial muscles up to a smile, bless her protective heart!"

2. My attacks on others. "Inevitably, I will have opinions

on various members of the flock I pastor, some of them negative at times. This doesn't mean I don't love them and desire the best for them, and God is able to adjust my opinions in the course of time, too. But when one person in a family lets off steam, pressure begins to build up in those who are listening. If I voice my personal misgivings about others to my wife or children, I no longer have any control over what those careless words will produce. Understand that my wife is not a gossip and is certainly not vindictive. My comments will taint her viewpoint, however, even if only slightly.

"Several years ago, we had a young Sunday school superintendent who I felt was not getting the job done. I told my wife about his mistakes, and I told her on numerous occasions how upset I was with him. Finally, God convicted me of being the one in the wrong, for I had not spent any time praying for and training the man. As I rectified this, he showed smooth progress in his ministry. My wife was not aware of this turnaround, however, and I noticed over a year later that she still had a critical attitude toward the man. The blame lay firmly on my shoulders. I apologized to her and asked her to forgive me for tainting this young man in her eyes. I also vowed inwardly to keep my most vindictive vents of steam to myself."

3. Ultra-sensitive issues. "With one of my college professors, it was common knowledge that if you asked him a question about black holes, even if it were only remotely connected to the topic at hand, he would wax eloquent on the subject, and the rest of the class would be history. We used to call him 'Black Hole Rollie.' We knew the topic that set him going. In the same way, I know the kinds of discussions that set my wife's mind buzzing. Each person, and each pastorate, has a different set of these terrible topics. For some of us, it may be learning of a church member's financial irresponsibility or doctrinal deviation. For others, hearing about even long-past sexual misconduct may create only unhealthy agitation. For still others, talking about how other people discipline their children gets the blood boiling.

"So Kathy and I have discovered that there are some issues

too sensitive to discuss — unless we've got a long, uninterrupted time together to fully process the topic. Ours are so sensitive I'm not even going to tell you what they are."

Phillips offers some help in discovering what those ultra-sensitive issues might be. You've probably found one when you uncover a topic that:

1. Contributes to obvious feelings of uneasiness in your spouse;

2. The two of you cannot constructively deal with;

3. You yourself feel uncomfortable discussing;

4. Leads to conversations whose long-term effect is only negative.

It takes time and mistakes to discover what these "don't tell me" issues are — for yourself and for your spouse.

These elements help a spouse have a healthy church experience. But perhaps the most critical element is developing a vital and authentic spiritual life as a family, the subject to which we now turn.

NINE

BUILDING SPIRITUAL LIFE TOGETHER

Children who know they are loved, know they have a purpose, and know they have a hope are prepared for anything this world wants to dish up.

TIM KIMMEL

If you have so much business to attend to that you have no time to pray, depend upon it, you have more business on hand than God ever intended you should have.

D. L. MOODY

Why is it that sublime inten-
tions often wind up looking ridiculous in reality? Even the
noblest intentions of a vital devotional life can wind up looking like tragi-comedy. Consider this pastor's description of
the bedtime prayer routine:

> With all the defiance of a mongrel whelp, my 4-year-old son
> stared me down and issued his answer: "No!" For the past
> four bedtimes, young John had become increasingly obstinate
> about praying.
> "You're going to pray if I have to wait here all night!"
> I heard myself utter this benign threat and had to wonder
> who let the crazy man in. What had happened to the wisdom
> of a hundred seminars on child rearing?
> But if John could play his role, I was going to get an Oscar
> for mine.
> "John, sit up and tell me what you want to pray for."
> John ignored me, and I panicked. Here I was, a pastor, a
> family counselor, a cherisher of boyhood memories, a cru-
> sader for handling children the right way. My jaw was tight,
> my lip curled, and above those was a top about to blow.

(Would God enter the scene with a pearl of wisdom or at least an off-stage prompt? Apparently not. So I improvised.)

"John, you always pray. Isn't there someone you would like to pray for?" (John pretends he is asleep.)

"John, Jesus likes it when you talk to him." (John emerges from Slumberland just long enough to yawn like a crevice.)

"John, I want you to pray right now." (John instantly turns onto his stomach.)

"Do you want Daddy to get the belt?" (Not even third-person rhetoric can shake the fever.)

"All right John, I'm leaving. I hope you have a horrible sleep." (Exit the spiritual father of two, dragging his tail and conscience behind him, agreeing with Bill Cosby that all 4-year-olds have brain damage.)

A number of parents can identify with this pastor's dilemma. They believe in the importance of spiritual training, but how to do it effectively? According to the LEADERSHIP survey, ministry homes are places where parents take seriously the task of growing spiritually *together*. When we asked, *Do you do anything consciously to build a spiritual life together as a family?* almost 86 percent of the pastors and spouses said yes. But their methods differed radically.

Here are some ways ministry families attempt to build a shelter for the spirit, soul, and body — or as Edith Schaeffer defines it, "an ecologically balanced environment."

Structured Times

Virtually every ministry family prays together, usually at meals, and most read Bible stories and pray with younger children at bedtime. "We pray with our children before they go to school in the morning, and we take time to listen and pray with the children before they go to bed," said one survey respondent.

Another pastor explained the benefits of the before-bedtime moments with his 6-year-old son: "It makes sure that I have an unhurried conversation with Kyle at least once a day. And that's important. Last week, as we finished reading and praying, I asked, as I usually do, 'Well, Kyle, what do you remember that happened today?'

" 'Mom got angry at me and didn't let me finish my lunch,' he said. When I asked what happened, he said his younger sister had yanked his soup bowl off the table, spilling it on the floor. He had pushed his sister away, knocking her down. His mother walked in just in time to see the mess and the push, and she banished Kyle to his room. 'But it wasn't my fault, Dad.'

"He needed to explain his side of things. And I explained that he should call his mother instead of push his sister. It was a good conversation. But if I hadn't taken the time to read and pray with him, I might have missed it. If I'd rushed in and asked, 'What happened today?' he'd have said, 'Nothing.' That's all you'll get if that's all the time you spend. Getting kids to be open with you takes time."

One benefit of a regular devotional time with the family is that, if unhurried and with the right atmosphere, it can build togetherness even within a busy family. Here are other ways of structuring times that have worked for pastoral families that responded to the survey.

"We try to sing hymns or Christian songs whenever we're in the car. This is an especially good discipline as we're driving to church on Sunday morning. It helps calm the frazzled nerves."

"We play a lot of tapes of Christian music. There are some great ones specifically for youngsters, and our kids love them."

"Our preschoolers faithfully watch some of the *Superbook* videos every day. These are animated Bible stories. We've bought some at Christian bookstores; others we've taped off the Christian TV station."

Several pastors mentioned using drama within the family. One missionary candidate wrote: "When Sarah, our toddler, would no longer sit still on Mommy's lap during family devotions, we had to think of some way to involve her. We decided to try acting out the story together. Soon Sarah, cloaked with a towel, was walking bent over and crying because she could not stand up straight, portraying the woman mentioned in Luke 13:10–13. I was Jesus, and told her, 'Be well!' as I put my hand on her. Immediately she stood up straight and began to shout, 'Hooray, I can stand up straight! I can stand up straight! Jesus healed me!' We no longer had a problem keeping Sarah involved."

A pastor from Chicago said, "We've been frustrated in our attempts to have a calm, orderly devotional time. Our three children range in age from 11 to 3, and their varying verbal and conceptual abilities make it almost impossible to do something that's meaningful for all. So the only thing we do as a whole family is to tell a Bible story occasionally, discuss it, and act it out.

"But our normal procedure is to read a story with our 11-year-old and pray with her, and then do the same thing separately with our two younger ones. We use The Picture Bible (David C. Cook) which presents the material in comic strip form. The kids enjoy seeing what the characters look like."

A structured family time is tough to make work. Many pastoral families no longer try — the struggle to interest every child every night seemed to be counterproductive. As one pastor said, "For a long time we felt bound to the family-altar concept, but finally realized it didn't work for us. We have, for the past few years, made a conscious effort to make our relationship with Christ a 'living way' — every situation becoming a normal opportunity to grow together spiritually. God is included in almost all conversations about every subject."

But others continue to feel it's worth the effort. Those who maintain the practice find three principles key:

The value of variety. David McDowell of College Church in Northampton, Massachusetts, says, "Anything done too many times, at least in our house, outlives its usefulness. Variety is essential. So sometimes we simply pray together; sometimes we'll have the older kids read to the younger ones;

sometimes we'll tell a Bible story or act one out; sometimes we'll go around the table and have each person tell about one kind deed given or received that day; other times we'll read from a devotional booklet."

Another pastor put it this way: "Don't try too hard. I never plan out a week's devotions for the family. Like the three princes of Serendip, we are just finding treasure along the way. However, like those picaresque princes, you do have to be searching to find treasure."

Avoid the teaching trap. One of the occupational hazards of ministry is taking our preaching/teaching role too seriously and not seeing ourselves as learners, especially with our children.

Psychiatrist Louis McBurney, who has counseled hundreds of pastors, says, "Some pastors never get out of the 'teacher' role. Most conversations with their children are devoted to telling their children what they need to know. That's why it was so refreshing to have Smith and Mary Helen Noland in our home. They had their 11-year-old son, Gregory, with them, and they consistently listened to him and invited him into the conversation. Rather than looking for things they could instruct him about, they asked him about his ideas and feelings. Gregory responded with relaxed confidence. The mutual respect was obvious."

Help children see that values are personal, not professional. You can tell a child, "We don't get drunk because we're Christians, the Bible says no, and besides, we're the pastoral family." None of those reasons may be strong enough, however, when peers suggest drinking and parents aren't around to enforce the family position.

Ministry families have found the more effective route is to discuss the world's values and their consequences, and then help the child form his or her own reasons for behavioral decisions. One of Jim Conway's daughters used to say when confronted with alcohol, "I've come up with ten reasons why I don't drink. The first is that it's fattening. . . ." Further down her list were reasons more "spiritual."

Many have found that family discussions about such issues need to start at least two years before children are confronted with the real thing. The regular family discussion and prayer time is one setting parents use to raise the issues: "Sometime down the road, kids are going to ask you what you believe about ____. Let's talk about it now. What do *you* want to stand for when such situations come up?" Such conversations bear far more fruit than do imposed expectations based on church roles.

When Things Break Down

Even with the best intentions, however, structured family times can fall apart. "Our regular daily devotions — reading a portion of Scripture and discussing it — were generally successful until our kids hit high school," wrote one pastor's wife. "With their busy schedules, our devotions broke down. We have more 'misses' than 'hits.' "

Another pastor said, "Last summer I took a three-month sabbatical, and the purpose of that time was to rest, to be together as a family, to do some traveling, and to expose ourselves to different churches and other Christian people. One of our other goals was to have a consistent devotional time together.

"And it worked. We all had our Bibles and notebooks, and before coming to breakfast, we'd each read the designated paragraph from the Gospel of Luke and jot our thoughts in our notebooks. Then we'd come together for breakfast and talk about what we'd read. It was the first time since the children had gotten older that we'd been able to do that on a regular basis. It was wonderful. So I said, 'There's no reason we can't keep doing this after we get back home.'

"But the minute we rolled into the driveway back home, it seemed like everyone took off in different directions. We had our morning devotions, I think, once in those next two months. Our breakfasts were just too rushed getting ready for school. Finally I gave up. Now we try to read something at suppertime, but in all honesty, we're doing well if we do that once a week.

"But we have been successful in encouraging the older kids to read the Bible and Christian books on their own. Our 16-year-old continues to keep a spiritual notebook. And I often ask them about what they're reading. We've had some helpful discussions."

The point is not to feel unduly guilty if a structured family devotional time doesn't come easily. The goal is to create an atmosphere in which focused attention on God is a natural part of life but not a tyranny.

"I tell my kids, and try to show with my life," says a minister in Virginia, "that we don't do this because it's the law, but because it helps us, and the older we get the more we realize we need it."

Unstructured Times

"I grew up in a home in which family devotions were rigidly observed, so we began that way," says David Seamands, former pastor and now professor at Asbury Seminary. "Well, with little children, devotions can be such bedlam you wonder if any spiritual value results. We were constantly disciplining the kids. Sometimes we just stopped, and then we had to get over the guilt of missing devotions. When the kids were teenagers, schedules were wild, and getting everyone together was impossible.

"Gradually, Helen and I began to see that table talk was just as important as a regular family altar. We began to major on this. We were able to have at least one meal a day together. At that meal we ran the whole day's events through a Christian sieve; everything that happened that day was discussed. I remember one meal where our oldest daughter, then about age 14, told about her first kiss. She could hardly wait to tell us. We were a very open family, and slowly, subtly, everything was dealt with in light of a Christian world view."

This perspective was a recurring theme among those

returning the LEADERSHIP surveys. For instance, one wrote: "Occasional Bible reading and a song after supper is a joy. But our emphasis is to build spiritual life naturally all day. God oozes throughout our family life rather than breaking in at one special devotional time."

For those who major on the unstructured, a few important principles stand out.

Be prepared for significant moments at unexpected times. Deborah Milam Berkley writes about her experience as a pastor's wife seeing God reveal himself to one of her children — and almost missing it because of the busyness of pastoral life.

Like young Samuel in Shiloh, 7-year-old Peter lived with a minister of God — in this case, his father, Jim. Also like young Samuel, when Peter first encountered the Lord, it was not at a moving worship service led by his father, nor during bedtime prayers. It was at 5:15 on a busy weekday evening, when both of his parents were unaware.

It had been a full day, and I was almost late for my evening swim. Pleased with my first athletic success (I was able to write my number of laps on the public record board!), I was eager for as much time in the pool as possible. Jim was running late for a church appointment.

We were relieved that our two children were ready to go and were quietly listening to music. As we hurriedly changed clothes, Peter came into our room with tears trickling down his cheeks.

"That song is making me cry," he said.

Jim mumbled something to the effect of "Oh, that's too bad," as he slipped past Peter and hurried out the door.

"Peter, I'm going to be late! Go back to the living room and wait," I said. But when his small form was gone, I started wondering if perhaps something was happening that was more important than swimming laps. So I called him back into the bedroom.

"Why is the song making you cry, Peter?" I asked.

"Well, it's the song about 'In my life, Lord, be glorified,' "

Peter sobbed, "and I just have a feeling like *I* want to be that way."

A thrill ran through me as I tipped up his face and looked into his eyes.

"Do you mean you want to glorify God in *your* life, like the song says?" When he nodded, I hugged him to me, grateful to God for not letting me ignore my son. Peter needed me to direct him to God, as Eli had done for Samuel. We prayed together, and Peter told God that he loved him and wanted to serve him. That evening we had a profoundly contented little boy at our house — and two very thankful parents.

But we almost missed it. Our adult priorities almost kept us from responding to Peter when he needed us. Since that time, I have tried to be better prepared to listen and to help.

Bring God into the daily events. One pastor said he was gratified to see his son apply spiritual lessons he's been taught. "One morning my wife burned her hand with hot oil making play dough. Our oldest son suggested that we pray before taking Mommy to the hospital. To this day, she has no scar — and guess who brags on God's healing power the most?"

Be open about both successes and struggles. Children can see both the joys and the trials of the Christian life, so many parents consciously walk both the high road and the low road with their children.

A Christian Reformed pastor's wife observed: "Our children need to know what is going on in our spiritual lives — our victories and our failures. Our kids became our prayer partners while they were still quite young. Some things were beyond them, but many could be shared in prayer. When children share spiritual struggles, they see our weaknesses and our sins, all the small and not-so-small failures that make up the walk of anyone who is serious about following Christ. But because they were spiritually involved with us, our inconsistencies weren't a stumbling block for them. It is much harder to be put off by your parents' sins when they admit them and you are helping them pray to overcome them.

"In the same way, our spiritual victories were not inflated out of proportion. They were seen as answers to prayer, things that can be achieved by anyone who is serious about letting God use him. When my daughters see my counsel help someone through a serious problem, or see someone introduced to Christ through my efforts, they are pleased, but not unduly impressed."

Take advantage of ministry opportunities. Says Mary Manz Simon, a Lutheran pastor's wife from Belleville, Illinois: "Our general rule is to accept assignments in the church at large that will allow at least the two of us and often our whole family to participate. For example, last summer we took some responsibility for an international gathering of Lutheran media missionaries in nearby St. Louis because our children would have a chance to meet people from around the world.

"Belleville is a rather closed, traditional community, and we wanted our kids to see what missionary ministry, the whole wider concept of sharing the gospel, was really about.

"One night we hosted men from nineteen countries at our home. They played T-ball in the backyard. One of the men from Brazil had never seen T-ball before. To this day, our son Matthew is convinced that he came to the United States just to play T-ball with him. The kids did a puppet show about sharing Jesus around the world. Our daughter Angela gave one of the men from France a pencil shaped like a cross, and every time we get a note from him he says, 'I'm using Angie's pencil.' Then, in our living room, our children got to hear them all sing 'What a Friend We Have in Jesus' in each of their native tongues. Our children will never forget that. We grew closer as a family and to the Lord that night."

Ministry as Family Tradition

As the Simons' example shows, somewhere between structured and unstructured approaches lies an important method many pastoral families capitalize on: developing a pattern of outreach. When children understand that ministry is rooted in a love for Christ and a desire to share that love with others, each event helps build a solid spiritual foundation.

Donald Bubna describes a tradition of hospitality his family developed while serving churches in San Diego and later in Salem, Oregon: "On Christmas Eve we would have a buffet in our home after the early Christmas Eve service for people who were alone. Christmas Day was our family celebration, but Christmas Eve was always an outreach event, and we'd invite people who needed it the most. That was part of our ministry as a family.

"As the children got older, we'd ask each child, 'Who do you want to invite this year?' And they would say, 'Let's have so-and-so. I don't know them very well' or 'I don't think so-and-so has anyplace to go.' At times, we would end up with strange combinations of people. But it was a rich time of ministry."

Now the Bubna children are grown and living on their own, but Don reports, "Last Christmas, we called our daughter, and she had put together a Christmas Eve buffet for some twenty people. Then we called our son who's in Alaska, and he'd had a group of people in, too, 'just like we always did, Dad.'

"As a parent, this is one of my greatest rewards: to see children freely choose to reach out to others by continuing, and building on, our family's tradition."

T E N

WHEN FAMILY TENSIONS AFFECT MINISTRY

The most irritating experience an artist can have is to have his work criticized before it is finished.

ANDREW WYETH

As we've seen, the ministry has an effect, both positive and negative, on a pastor's family life. But the converse is also true: family life can have a profound effect on ministry. In the next three chapters, we'll look at the burdens and benefits that family relationships can bring to ministry.

One of the toughest burdens can be family tensions. Consider the story of this pastor from California:

We were eating lunch in a favorite Chinese restaurant. My son was nineteen, good looking, and engaged to an attractive woman four years his senior, whom he had met at Bible college. We thought he was too young for marriage and had expressed our concern. "Give yourself and your relationship more time to mature," we said. But when you're nineteen and the future spreads before you . . .

"Dad, we're going to have a baby."

Time stood still.

"I'm sorry to hurt you like this. We're going to get married right away."

We sat quietly, picking at food, grasping for thoughts. An image flashed through my mind: our son's future, in the form of water and sludge, rushing down an open drain. *Pull yourself together*, I told myself. I excused myself from the table to make a phone call. Then I dialed the church office and spoke in controlled tones to the familiar voice at the other end so as not to betray the inner turmoil.

"Kill the announcement of my new sermon series, will you? I've been having some second thoughts."

"I'm sorry, Pastor. It's already gone to press."

"Okay," I replied after a moment. "I'll deal with it later. Please let my wife know that I've had lunch with our son and we'll be leaving for home in a few minutes. It is important for her to meet us there. We have some things we need to discuss."

Walking slowly back to the table, my thoughts kept coming back to the sermon series I'd intended to begin this Sunday: "The Future Family." What timing! What could I say when I was still reeling from my own family's situation?

I told my son and his bride-to-be that I felt the need to tell the church board about the situation. They wanted to meet with the board as well, but I said no. As I reflected later, that was probably a mistake. They should have been permitted to share personally. After all, it was their marriage and their baby. But I was in a protectionist mood. Their problem had become my problem.

Our board of five gathered for the specially called meeting. I shared with them the news. "If even one of you feels this would be too much for the church family to absorb, I will understand and tender my resignation," I said. I explained how important we felt it was for us to stand with our son and his fiancée if they were to have any chance for a successful future. If that meant resigning, then that's the way it would have to be.

To a person, the board members affirmed both me and our family. One reminded me of how I had stood with him in a similar crisis some years before. Another offered understanding because he faced similar temptation as a young man. We prayed and cried together.

It was a small May wedding. After a brief honeymoon, my son and his wife went to live with her parents, in order to get on their feet financially. Six weeks later, after an explosive and embarrassing confrontation with her parents, they spent the next thirty days in our home while we went on vacation. Much of our motivation in leaving was to permit the newlyweds some privacy. Soon after our return, they rented an apartment.

In November, our daughter was married. Her wedding was large and beautiful. At the conclusion of the rehearsal dinner (an event my son had not included), my son wistfully commented, "This is really a lot different than our wedding, isn't it?"

Two weeks later, on Thanksgiving Day, we became grandparents of a beautiful baby girl. The excited father and mother proudly showed off their little miracle. It seemed that, at long last, things might be coming together.

They smiled and laughed when visiting us. We enjoyed our time together. But their apartment gradually became a war zone of angry words aimed to bring the greatest pain. Already unsure of themselves, they felt the pressure mounting of "forever" entrapment. When a terrible mistake has been made, is there ever relief?

She dealt with conflict by going home to mother. He internalized the anger — and began to drink. As the pain increased, so did the number of drinks.

In the church, loving support was given by many, probably too many. Church members reached out to the young couple, but she could not trust the voices because they came from "his father's congregation." He could not accept the voices because they seemed like multiple parents. It was like having hundreds of close relatives, never knowing when one would step up with a word of wisdom. And, of course, there was always the underlying guilt and embarrassment of having conceived out of wedlock. People might not say much about that. But what must they be thinking?

Our son knew he had let his parents down. They had forgiven — at least that's what they said — but in his mind, he was the black sheep, maybe even the lost sheep. It became impossible to measure up to expectations, both real and imagined. The couple began to hate the church, this loving, but impossible Parent.

At first our son sold cars, then burglar systems. Finally he took a position with an aircraft firm. She worked in a restaurant and sold art objects on the side. Together they struggled with financial problems — and increasing hopelessness.

We tried to help when it seemed appropriate, but we did our best to stay out of the way as well. What our relationship with them should be became increasingly difficult to determine. They both began coming to us for counsel, little suggestions and encouragement. They kept looking for that word of wisdom their pastor/parents always seemed to have for everyone else. But when is one's counsel that of concerned parent and when that of impartial pastor? We were never sure. Even on my most objective day, a "word of wisdom" may not feel objective to the respective in-law. We assisted financially with professional Christian marriage counseling, but even this became suspect, because the psychologist was a friend of his family.

One day the phone rang. Our son's voice cracked with emotion. He had come home that day to find both his wife and their daughter gone. After he'd left for work that morning, her parents had helped her move back with them. Everything she had brought into their life was gone: the baby, the furniture, the pictures, the wedding gifts from her side of the family. What remained was in a heap in the center of the apartment. On top lay a carefully wrapped birthday gift — and a note saying she wanted a divorce.

That evening we sat quietly around the dining room table.

Twenty-one candles burned low on the birthday cake. No one felt like singing, "Happy Birthday."

The following spring, the divorce papers were signed. Three months later, she remarried.

Our son moved in with us, and on the surface, it appeared we were back to square one.

Then one day, he announced he had resigned from the aircraft company to start his own business. That's what he'd always wanted to do, he said. Now it was time. He was receiving lots of encouragement from a young lady in our church whom he had been seeing. Her parents were supportive of the idea, too, and assured him he could do anything he really set his mind to do. He opened a home repair and remodeling business. He loved working with wood and was quite good at it. Jobs started coming in. Things were looking up once more.

But his relationship with the young lady seemed to be moving too rapidly. Once again, we found ourselves watching from the sidelines with a growing anxiety. It appeared to be the classic rebound relationship. He disagreed. So did the parents of the young lady. I met with them after church one evening. We spoke at length about the future of our children, but we went away with greatly divergent views of the situation.

Then came the announcement: they were to be married the following April — a big church wedding, even a rehearsal dinner.

The rising tension at home finally boiled over one Sunday before I left for the first service. What we were able to say about this new relationship was not what our son was able to receive. He felt if things didn't change between us . . . well, they just had to change. Our voices got louder. At one point I wondered if he would actually hit me.

I told him the time had come to make living arrangements elsewhere. The tension in our home was too high; we were stretched as far as we could go. He listened in cold anger, then said he would be gone before I arrived home from church.

As I drove away, I thought, *I'm on my way to church. I'm supposed to bring inspiration and strength to God's people. But we're losing our son. Life is out of control. When was the last time any of us were really happy?*

"Good morning everyone!" I said minutes later. "Welcome. Let's stand and sing Hymn 415. . . ."

Many pastors are familiar with the feeling of trying to minister while knowing things are not good at home. While conditions in other homes may not have deteriorated to the degree they did in the story above, most ministry families have their share of tensions. As one pastor said, "My toughest sermon was the time I had to speak on love the morning after an argument with my wife."

Another said, "I can barely preach if I've gotten angry with my children on the way to church. It's hard to talk about forgiveness when I need to practice some."

Family relationships, if strained, can hinder a person's ability to minister, but many church leaders have learned that ministry can — and must — continue even when conditions at home are less than optimal. Every family will face times of turbulence.

Perhaps one of the most prominent examples of persistent ministry in the face of domestic turmoil is John Wesley.

Before his marriage at age 47, Wesley had at least two romantic interests that ended in disappointment. In Georgia, teenager Sophie Hopkey grew tired of waiting for young Wesley to commit himself; she married another man, and Wesley's angry reaction brought an end to his ministry in America. Back in England, Wesley's sporadic courtship of Grace Murray ended abruptly when she hastily married Methodist lay-preacher John Bennet at the urging of Charles Wesley. Charles was convinced his brother's marriage to Grace would have been a terrible mistake, so he falsely convinced Grace that John had decided to give her up. Wesley was deeply wounded. He wrote to his friend Thomas Bigg,

"Since I was six years old, I have never met with such a severe trial. . . . The whole world fought against me; but above all my own familiar friend."

Shortly thereafter, Wesley apparently fell in love with a widow named Molly Vazeille. After preaching one Sunday in February 1751, he slipped on the ice crossing London Bridge and hurt his ankle. He was taken to Mrs. Vazeille's house, where he spent the remainder of the week "partly in prayer, reading and conversation, partly in writing an *Hebrew Grammar* and *Lessons for Children*" — an unusual courtship. The next Sunday he preached kneeling, and the next day he married Molly Vazeille.

It was probably the worst mistake of Wesley's life. "Whatever Molly Vazeille's defects, and they may not be glossed over, Wesley must bear some responsibility for [the marriage's] ultimate failure," writes Wesley biographer V. H. H. Green. "Molly Vazeille was no starry-eyed young girl, enraptured by the divinely sent evangelist. She was a widow with experience of marriage and four grown-up children who had no desire to become part of a traveling caravan."

As soon as his foot healed, Wesley was off on his travels. Molly tried accompanying him, and at first, Wesley commended her: "They talk of you much and know not how to commend you enough, even for your plainness of dress, your sitting among the poor at preaching, your using sage-tea (Wesley had strong views about the bad effects of green tea), and not being delicate in your food." But the rough roads, bad weather ("This day," Wesley once wrote, a bit smugly but no doubt sincerely, "I was wet from morning to night with the continued rain, but I found no manner of inconvenience"), shabby inns, and poor food were too much for the former merchant's wife. She stopped traveling with him and stayed home, brooding on her perceived mistreatment.

She questioned his affection. When they were together, they exchanged angry words. She began to doubt his fidelity. She found some letters that aroused intense jealousy.

Finding little support at home, Wesley had taken to writing

Sarah Ryan, a woman he had appointed housekeeper at Kingswood School, and at times his words were indiscrete: "Conversing with you, either by speaking or writing, is an unspeakable blessing to me. I cannot think of you without thinking of God."

When Molly found out about Sarah, who was twenty years younger than the 54-year-old Wesley, her anger increased. She discovered Sarah's checkered past. (As a young woman, Sarah had been a domestic servant and married a corkcutter who was, in fact, already married. When the corkcutter deserted Sarah, she wed an Irish sailor named Ryan, and while he was at sea, she bigamously married an Italian. Eventually Ryan sailed to America, and the Italian joined the British navy, leaving Sarah to return to domestic service. It was then that she heard Wesley preach and was converted.)

When Molly found in Wesley's pocket a letter addressed to Sarah, she angrily observed, "The whore now serving you has three husbands living."

The marriage did not survive. Molly turned increasingly vindictive before the final separation. Wesley wrote of "being continually watched over for evil . . . hearing a thousand little, tart, unkind reflections in return for the kindest words I could devise." Another time he wrote, "My wife picks my lock and steals my private papers." She published his indiscretions and defamed him to his critics. In one celebrated incident, she accosted Wesley while he was speaking and tried to drag him away by his hair. He once said she could undo in two minutes more than he could do in two weeks.

For another twenty years, he hoped for the possibility of reconciliation, but in his last surviving letter, dated October 2, 1778, he doubted whether they would meet again in this world: "If you were to live a thousand years, you could not undo the mischief that you have done. And till you have done all you can toward it, I bid you farewell."

She died three years later, but Wesley did not know of her death for several days and did not attend the funeral.

Certainly the responsibility for the tensions in the Wesley

household rests with both John and Molly. When they were married, he was already wed — to his mission. He wasn't prepared to focus his energies on family concerns. He was certainly no model husband. For her part, Molly became increasingly unbalanced and jealous, and certainly her determination to defame her husband was inexcusable.

But perhaps the greatest lesson to emerge from this story is simply the fact that hardly anyone has heard it. John Wesley has not been judged by history for his failure at home but for his accomplishments in ministry.

Despite the turmoil at home, Wesley unarguably had a tremendous impact throughout England. He traveled more than 250,000 miles on horseback, preached 46,000 sermons (a thousand times a year), wrote 400 books, established hundreds of societies, and founded schools, hospitals, and orphanages. He not only helped change the moral climate of eighteenth century England (he was an important influence on William Wilberforce, a key figure in abolishing slavery throughout the British Empire), but Wesley's influence continues into the twentieth century (seen not only in the Methodist and Wesleyan denominations, but also in the thousands of small-group Bible studies that trace their spiritual lineage to the "bands" formed by the methodical Wesley to promote Bible study).

Ministry is indeed possible even when family tensions present unavoidable challenges. At times the tensions are a result of our own poor choices — and our responsibility is to right whatever wrongs we've committed as much as we are able. Other times the tensions are the result of other people's decisions or circumstances beyond our control. In either case, two principles help point the way to the place where, by God's grace, effective ministry can still happen.

Accepting and Admitting Shortcomings

The first principle is to accept and admit the tensions family life produces.

In a LEADERSHIP interview, I once asked family-life advocate James Dobson about the inevitable gap between public ministry and private family life. How does a minister encourage family life publicly when he knows things are stressful at home?

Dobson said, "If you don't have your home life in good order, you have no business teaching others how to handle theirs; on the other hand, *no one* is perfect at home.

"You can no more be a perfect father or husband than you can be a perfect human being. You may know all the rules for good family life, all the biblical principles — and yet simple fatigue will affect your ability to implement them at certain times.

"So after a sermon it is *always* possible for a pastor's wife to say to her husband on the way home, 'I guess you know you don't live up to what you preached today.' That is the nature of human imperfection."

I asked, "Does Shirley ever remind you that you're talking further than you've walked?"

"She is generous to me because she loves me, but it's not difficult for her to identify my faults," he said. "That's why I frequently talk publicly about my shortcomings at home. In one of my books I describe our classic 'umbrella fight.' I'd come home from a trip exhausted. Shirley wanted me to clean the back yard umbrella that Saturday, while I felt entitled to watch a football game. After all, I'd been working hard and deserved a day off. But while I was out of town, she had been taking care of our children and managing the family. Now that I was home, she felt it was high time I offered her some relief. We had a three-day collision of wills over that.

"I think it's important for family specialists to reveal incidents like that. I have also tried to describe times I did not father our children properly. Chuck Swindoll is careful to admit the same kind of faults. We need to admit we're not perfect at home. Honesty demands it. And people respond to that openness.

"With one group, I told about a frustrating day when I

really rode the backs of my children. I said, 'That day I violated everything I write about.' The audience applauded. They need to hear about times I haven't measured up to my own standard."

Hanging in There

The second principle is simply to hang in there long enough to see if God's grace is sufficient to let the ministry continue.

Steve Harris is a pastor who knows family tension of a different sort. His son, Matthew, was born with spina bifida and an unnerving complication, apneic spells, in which Matthew would suddenly stop breathing and have to be resuscitated — as many as twenty times a day. The doctors, unable to explain the exact cause or treatment, warned Steve and his wife, Pam, that the next spell could end Matthew's life.

"We never know when Matthew might stop breathing and never go anywhere without our medical equipment to help revive him," writes Steve. "Our current estimate is that Matthew has stopped breathing and nearly died over 2,780 times. A parishioner once suggested that 'by now you're probably used to it.' I wish that were true. Each spell is as frightening as the first, as we anxiously watch, wait, and wonder if we truly are witnessing the end of Matthew's life."

Matthew's medical problems have made ministry — indeed, life itself — a daily challenge. Steve has felt keenly the various emotions that make ministry so difficult for a hurting pastor. But he has learned to minister despite the stressful family situation.

" 'One of the most important lessons you can learn,' a professor told me in seminary, 'is that at times, you'll have to minister when you don't feel like it.' Those times have certainly come," says Steve.

"On a warm July morning I was scheduled to perform a wedding, but right beforehand, Matthew suffered five serious apneic spells within an hour. As I dressed for the wedding in the hospital men's room, the last place I wanted to be was celebrating with a young couple anticipating the joys of married life. But I also knew I had made a commitment. The wedding went fine, although I'm sure I've done better."

The fact he did it at all was a positive accomplishment. The decision to "hang in there" is an important step for any pastor.

Yes, family tension affects ministry, but as John Wesley, James Dobson, and Steve Harris have learned, it doesn't prevent it. At times, however, it does demand certain crucial responses, to which we turn in the next chapter.

ELEVEN

WHEN A CHILD STRAYS

Children are strange possessions. We raise them so we can lose them.

M. O. VINCENT

Not long ago I was at an informal gathering of ministers when the conversation turned to disciplining children. Two of the pastors got into a spirited discussion about how they were raised — and how they were raising their own children.

"This will sound weird to you guys," said one pastor, "but my dad never laid a hand on me — ever. I remember one instance in particular: we had a long driveway, and when Dad would take his Sunday afternoon nap, I liked to drive the car up and down the driveway. Sometimes, to be cool, I'd open the car door to see where I was going as I backed up. But once I got too close to the house, and I caught the door on the porch steps and nearly ripped the door off its hinges. I remember how frightened I was, but Dad came out, looked things over, and said, 'I think we can fix it.' "

Another pastor said, "That's not the way my dad would have reacted!"

Amid the laughter, a third pastor said, "A few weeks ago, my 11-year-old son was riding his bike to school, and on the way he stopped at the dirt track with a few of his buddies. He figured, *Hey, I've got my lunch; I've got my bike; why go to school?*

By the time he got home, I'd discovered where he had been, but I didn't bring it up immediately. I wanted to see what he would say. So I asked, 'How was school today?' He said, 'It was okay.'

" 'What if I knew for a fact that you weren't in school today,' I asked. 'What would you think then?'

"He put his head down and said, 'I think I'm dead meat.' And he was!' "

While we all laughed, I was struck by the different responses parents make to children's misdeeds. Some parents are more authoritarian, emphasizing respect rather than intimacy. Others are more democratic, emphasizing participation and feeling close.

No style, however, is guaranteed to prevent a child from rebelling. A child may rebel because of too much control or too little. Ministry families are not immune to this rebellion. Indeed, since family relationships affect ministry so greatly, many pastors struggle with the proper response to children who stray.

Let's look at the range of children's misbehavior and how it affects ministry.

Degrees of Disobedience

Misdeeds range from minor to major but fall into four categories.

Mischief. Some misbehavior is relatively minor and a normal part of growing up. "Our church is too small to have a children's church," said one pastor's wife. "So the kids are in the worship service with us. I get frustrated with a child who pipes up in the middle of the sermon, 'I'm bored.' So I have a bag stocked with baseball cards, Cheerios, coloring books, and puzzles. Even with these diversions, our children occasionally disrupt the service, and I have to remove them. But I have to remember they are kids first and pastors' kids about fifth."

Most pastors have learned to handle such minor "kids' stuff" with a few simple guidelines.

1. Let children know what is expected before the situation arises. One pastor's 4-year-old repeatedly tried to get to the platform during the service — by crawling under the pews. He had to learn when he could and could not roam freely in the sanctuary.

2. If children need correction, try not to embarrass them publicly, especially not in front of their friends.

"We practice the 1-2-3 rule," said a pastor's wife. "I'll look at the child who's misbehaving and let him know I disapprove of what he's doing. Then I'll count to three, either verbally or by raising my fingers. If the behavior hasn't stopped by the count of three, I act, usually by making him sit by himself, or if necessary by removing him from the scene and disciplining him privately."

3. In public, hold your children to the same standards of behavior as you would other people's children. "I am teaching confirmation class right now to a group that includes my daughter," said the pastor of an Evangelical Covenant Church. "As junior highers are sometimes, she was squirmy, so I had to say, 'Sandy, settle down. Let's get back to work and not be so silly.' I would have said the same thing to any other kid in the class."

4. Offer reasons for correction based on what's "right and wrong," what's "loving or unloving," what's "wise or foolish" — never "because Daddy is a pastor" or "because of what people will think." One pastor has buttressed his determination not to do that by trying to eliminate the embarrassment factor: "I've said up front, 'At times my kids will embarrass me — they're normal kids — but please let them be kids and try to help me be a parent.'

"I find I tend to overdiscipline when I feel embarrassed. I recently came down way too hard on my son for being rambunctious in the foyer after church. It was because he was embarrassing me, the pastor. I apologized to him afterward. I'm trying to accept the fact that kids occasionally will embarrass you. Our people can accept that; now I'm trying to."

What effect does a child's mischief have on ministry? Most ministry families said, "No effect," and a few said the occasions when they'd had to correct their children had been a positive time of ministry.

"It made my husband's ministry more human," said one pastor's wife in Maryland. "As people saw him dealing successfully with his children, they were more willing to approach him for help."

Questionable Choices. Slightly more serious than mischief are decisions that make parents squirm. For instance, kids' deciding they don't want to go to church.

On the LEADERSHIP survey, no one recommended telling the children, "We have to go because we're church leaders." Instead, the emphasis was on obedience to Christ or, on occasion, because it's a distinctive of our family.

David McDowell, who pastors College Church in Northampton, Massachusetts, smiles when telling about one encounter: "We were on our way to the car when our 10-year-old started whining, 'I don't want to go to church. I want to stay home and watch TV.' I decided to be firm. I pointed my finger at him and said with as much thunder in my voice as I could muster, 'You are the first and last McDowell ever to complain about going to church.' That was three years ago, and I haven't had to say anything since."

At the same time, another Massachusetts pastor said, "As our kids were growing up, we didn't want them to feel the church is an intrusion. We wanted them to know their lives were not inextricably intertwined with the church and that the validity of dad's ministry did not hang on their performance. We never required them to be in all the programs. In fact, there were Sunday nights when I said, 'Why don't you stay home tonight? You've had a rough weekend.' But nineteen times out of twenty both would say, 'No, we're going to church.' "

Yet another pastor's daughter announced she was going to the youth group at a different church because her girl friend went there, and she didn't like some of the people where her dad pastored.

"That was sticky," said her father. "I didn't care if people gasped at the pastor's kid going to another church. But I didn't want my daughter running from relational issues she needed to address, so we compromised. I eventually let her go to events at the other church, but she had to attend at least half the youth events in our church. It worked out well."

Other questionable choices center on lifestyle issues. One Kentucky pastor describes such a situation: "Our 15-year-old daughter announced one day that she was going to the school dances, which we knew would raise eyebrows in our church. That was the first time our philosophy of freedom of choice was really put to the test. We sat and talked through all the issues as I saw them. She said, 'I know all that, but I still want to go.' So with fear and trepidation, we backed her freedom to make this choice. She went to three or four, and then one night she came home early. I said, 'What's going on?' To our great joy, she told us she'd made another decision: 'Oh, Daddy, those just aren't my kind of kids.' And that was the end of it."

A third area of questionable choices is in rejecting certain parts of their spiritual upbringing. "I remember when our son came home from science class one day and told us that Genesis was wrong and that evolution was a better explanation of origins," said a pastor. "I knew this was partly for shock effect, so I decided to allow for his disagreement. It led to some good conversations. With some kids, you let them see they're special to you by allowing them to be different. Most preachers' kids are too smart to be real prodigals. They know the life of a prodigal is a dead-end street, so the only way to get a minister parent's attention is to disagree on religious matters. The trick is not to over-react."

Other pastors have found it helpful to identify whether the

questionable choice is an isolated incident or part of a pattern. If it's a single instance, most tend to be lenient, but if it's part of a pattern, they're more likely to intervene.

"I've been helped by the analogy of a fence," said one pastor. "Parental intervention is like a fence post — that's where the direction of the fence will change, if necessary. But between the fence posts, you've got the rails running long enough to see what direction the fence is going. Generally the older kids get, the further the intervals between fence posts."

Extended Conflict. As they grow, children almost inevitably come into areas of conflict with their parents. This is as true for pastors as for anyone else. Sometimes the conflict is low-key; other times it's sharp and intense. Listen as one pastor describes life with his teenage daughter:

Late spring of her sixth-grade year, it was as if Wendy came out of her bedroom one day and said, "I'm going to ruin your lives for the next four years." Overnight she became strong-willed and argumentative.

Of course, she was worried about her appearance, going into junior high, and hormonal changes that she (and I) didn't understand. Knowing that didn't make the situation easier; it just compounded my wondering how to respond.

She was moody; she didn't want to eat dinner with us; she spent hours in her bedroom alone. That summer on vacation, she wanted to do her thing first and then go back to the hotel; she didn't want to let anybody else do what they wanted to do. It was so awful I called my mother and apologized for whatever hell I had put her through.

Every statement was an absolute: "I'm never going to school again." "I'm not going to talk to that person ever again." Because I'm a driving sort of individual, that set up many head-to-head battles. For example, I'd ask, "Where do you want to go for supper?"

"I don't care."

"Fine. I'll decide."

In the car, she'd ask, "Where are we going?"

"McDonald's."

"I refuse to eat there. I want to go to Burger King."

"I asked you, and you said you didn't care, so I made the decision. The next time I ask, please tell me and we'll go to Burger King, but tonight we're going to McDonald's."

"Then I'm not eating!"

It was difficult for me to discuss this with people in the congregation. My wife and I saw a counselor — one who I had referred other people to many times. That was hard admitting we needed help. But I did manage to talk about my fears and anguish with perhaps fifteen people.

What surprised me was that the more we shared, the more we found out some of the "model kids" of our church were like Wendy at home. One lay leader, whose son is a leader in the youth group, told me there were times when he and his son wouldn't speak for days at a time. I never would have known.

When I did mention this to some of the elders, one said, "If you want my daughter to invite your daughter over for the weekend just to give you guys some rest, please let us do it."

When another of our elders moved in across the street, we felt the freedom to tell him and his wife, "If you see Wendy smoking, don't feel you have to hide it from us. We know she smokes, and she takes walks sometimes because we won't let her smoke in the house." They were most understanding.

When Wendy shaved the right side of her head, I never said a word, but it ate me up inside. When I told a fellow pastor about our situation, he, a Nazarene, comforted me with a story of his own: "A lady came up to me recently and said, 'Thanks for letting your daughter dress the way you do. My parents wouldn't let me express myself when I was growing up.' " That helped.

We also learned to see the humor in our situation. A pastor friend used us as a sermon illustration: "I know a guy whose daughter just dyed her hair orange. That's probably kind of stupid, but since when is being stupid grounds for not getting into the church? As my friend says, 'I don't know why they're upset about my daughter's orange hair. Some of the little old ladies in our church have blue hair.' "

The whole process really deepened my love for my wife, Sara, because we were in it together. We realize how kids can ruin a marriage because we had times when we would snap at each other. We had to keep saying, "We're not the enemy," and keep renewing and reviewing our love.

It also made me more sensitive to single parents; I don't know how they get through it. The other day at a soccer game a single parent from our church was talking to Sara and me about how her son is belching all the time now. And how he bought a new toilet seat and cover — the top of it is this big yellow and black sign that says, DANGER. You lift the cover, and it says, FARTING ZONE. That's being a 13-year-old boy, but this poor woman doesn't understand that, and she doesn't have anybody to talk to.

So we've been talking about launching a Parents of Adolescents Anonymous, where we get together and say, "Everything said in this room will be confidential. We're going through it together." One day in the adult Sunday school class, we broke into small groups, and Sara was in such pain she described some of it. Bob and Jenny, the couple she talked with, said, "You've got to pray for us. We're living through the same things." So it's drawn us closer together, deepened our faith. We realize we've got to pray like crazy, because nothing we've tried is going to change our daughter.

When such conflict erupts in a ministry home, the stress level heightens. But two understandings have helped keep parents from overreacting.

First, a certain amount of rebellion is necessary and healthy. Donald Miller, who grew up in a pastor's home, said he didn't go through a time of serious rebellion ("although like many young persons, there were some erratic periods in my service for Christ as I grew up"), but he noted that nonrebellion also has its negative side.

"If there's a danger in having a father you highly respect and nearly worship," he said, "it's that you may accept his views without checking their validity for yourself."

Second, keeping calm is perhaps the most important statement you can make. One pastor was discouraged because of his son's negative attitude toward church. A wise elder took him aside and said, "Paul, when your kids are moving into adolescence and you panic, it says all the wrong things. It says you don't believe in them, and you don't believe in God."

The elder went on to say, "I spent some time with your son this week, and he's going to be okay. He just needs some room to grow." The pastor said later, "You can't imagine what a comfort those words were."

Serious Straying. Some children do more than simply disagree with their parents; they turn their backs on them — and reject their values. These situations cause particular pain.

When the LEADERSHIP survey asked, *Have you ever had a child seriously stray?* overall, 14 percent of the ministry families said yes. But when you don't count those with young children or no children, the figure is higher. Of those who had children 18 and older, 30 percent said they've had at least one child seriously stray. Of course, many of these families had other children who did not seriously stray. And to further put this in perspective, we mustn't forget that more than two-thirds of the pastoral families surveyed who had grown children did not face serious rebellion.

But 30 percent did, and even one child who strays dominates parents' attention and strains other family relationships. Open rebellion, spiritual straying, or obviously bad choices not only cause parents deep grief, but threaten to undermine their entire ministry.

Evangelist Dwight L. Moody had a special concern because his oldest son, Will, was cool to spiritual matters. Once he wrote Will a revealing letter: "I have not talked much with you for fear I would turn you more and more against Him, whom I love more than all the world, and if I have ever said or done anything unbecoming a Christian father I want you to forgive me. . . . I have always thought that when a mother and father are Christians and their children were not that there was something decidedly wrong with them. I still think so. . . . If I thought I had neglected to do my duty toward my three children I would rather die than live." Many parents in ministry understand the feeling.

In Moody's case, the story had a happy ending. The following year Will made a profession of faith. When Dwight heard of it, he wrote, "I do not think you will ever know until you have a son of your own how much good it did me to hear this."

Not all stories end that way. What about children who do *not* wind up reconciling with their parents or with God? Does that mean ministry is over?

The answer from pastors I surveyed and interviewed was overwhelmingly *no*. They were nearly unanimous in agreeing that effective ministry can — and in most cases should — continue even if children rebel.

They identified three overriding principles that guide a parent in ministry when children stray.

Unconditional Love

Children need to know that our love for them is forever, whenever, and with no strings attached. Although we expect them to live the kind of lives God wants them to live, they must know that should they fail, we would still accept them. Parents agreed this should be put into words so children do not doubt it.

Writes a pastor's wife: "One of our daughters always had a high consciousness of sin, and she kept talking about her fear of going to jail. We explained that even if she did something that put her in jail, she would still be our daughter, and we would love her just as much as if it had never happened. We told her that just as God never stops loving us no matter what we do, we would never stop loving her, either. I might feel terrible and cry a lot, but I would visit her in jail just as I would if she were in the hospital. With a big smile she said, 'You would?' That was the assurance she needed. She never brought up the subject of going to jail again."

Such love tells children they don't have to test their parents with far-out behavior to see whether they'll still be accepted. Although this is important for all parents, it's more so for church leaders, whose children realize their behavior could threaten the parent's ministry. If they feel ministry is more important to us than their welfare, they may yield to the temptation to act in some socially unacceptable way to force their parents' hand.

An Unmanaged Household?

One of the fears of pastors is that a child's behavior will render their entire ministry invalid. A few oft-cited Bible verses make any family in ministry uncomfortable.

"An elder must be blameless . . . a man whose children believe and are not open to the charge of being wild and disobedient" (Titus 1:6).

"If anyone does not know how to manage his own family, how can he take care of God's church?" (1 Tim. 3:5).

In addition, there's the tragic example of Eli, whose two sons desecrated the temple, and as a result God condemned all three (1 Sam. 2:22–36).

What does this mean for people in ministry today? Does a son or daughter who strays render a minister disqualified? Here are the responses of a number of pastors and denominational officials.

"My response is no," says Donald Njaa, who oversees credentials for ministers in the Evangelical Covenant Church. "The rebellion may well be not against the father or mother; it may be a rebellion against the pressure they've been put under by the church."

"The Timothy passage concludes with a warning not to fall into reproach, and the greatest reproach is hypocrisy —

when something is espoused in the pulpit but not upheld in the home," says Mike Halcomb, a denominational official with the Conservative Congregational Christian Conference. "But that passage is not referring to the normal maturation process of children. Our boys were inclined to pillage and plunder, sometimes in the church basement! I had to reprimand them. But I trust their being normal boys doesn't disqualify me for ministry. I also don't think the passage speaks to grown children (and in Bible days, that would probably be 14 to 16 years old) who choose to dissociate themselves from the faith."

Other ministers, while acknowledging the tragic example of Eli, point out that Samuel's sons also were rebellious, but Samuel's leadership remained intact. And while Cain was a murderer, God didn't hold his father, Adam, accountable.

As pastor Charles Swindoll has said, "There's been only one perfect Father, and even he has a lot of wayward kids."

"We've known pastoral families where a child has been wild and rebellious," says a pastor's wife, "and yet as far as we could tell, the parents did everything they could to bring up that child to love the Lord. Many times, five or six years later, that child will come back to faith, and to love and respect the parents." In other words, why should a parent's ministry end because of a child's temporary insanity?

Eugene Peterson, pastor of Christ Our King Presbyterian Church in Bel Air, Maryland, says, "There are many possible reasons for children's not growing up in the faith. I have three kids, all grown. One of them had an extremely difficult adolescence. Now she's wonderful, and our two sons coming after never knew adolescence was anything but praising God. But when our daughter was in trouble, people in the congregation were gracious. I was grateful they didn't say, 'Peterson, you must be doing something terrible at home because your daughter's acting this way.' "

Perhaps the congregation's attitude is the key to determining whether ministry can continue when a child strays. They're the ones observing whether the home is managed or unmanaged in the midst of difficulty.

After hearing Eugene Peterson's story, Charles Swindoll observed, "Eugene, it was because you have integrity that your congregation surrounded you. You had endeared yourself to those people, and not even the waywardness of a willful daughter could drive a wedge between them and you. Had you been covering up, had you been obviously alienating your family, I wonder if the congregation would have said, 'Let's stand by him no matter what.' They knew the most grieved person in the church was the pastor. That's managing a family. There was a caring attitude, a consistency and integrity that showed in your grief when a daughter turned away for a time."

Directed Independence

Whether the parenting style tends to be strict or lenient, the goal of the parenting process is the same: to raise a child who will one day be able to make mature decisions for himself or herself. No parent wants a child to remain dependent upon Mom and Dad for a lifetime. Christian parents desire their children to be able to live independently, and also to make a free choice to follow Christ.

M. O. Vincent, a pastor's son who now has four children of his own, observed reflectively, "Children are strange possessions. We raise them so we can lose them."

In a sense, parenting is one form of the Christian practice of discipling — helping bring another person to maturity.

Many ministry parents find helpful *remembering that God is ultimately responsible* for the salvation and sanctification of his children. That takes some of the pressure off them — and their children.

"None of the four kids in my family went through a significant period of rebellion. For that I must give a small share of credit to covenant theology," writes Tim Stafford, the son of a Presbyterian pastor. He specifically points to the belief that a child, if raised in the nurture and admonition of the Lord, is not a small representative of Satan in urgent need of reclaiming, but a beginning Christian.

"Though it is necessary for the child, as for all Christians, to renounce sin and to throw himself on the mercy of God, a proper Presbyterian parent does not look on his child as an outsider to God's grace. He believes that the Holy Spirit can be as unobstructed in a child's life as in his own. This does a lot to reduce tension in the home. It reduces the pressure on the child to make a radical reversal in order to avoid falling into hell. It merely calls on the child to continue in the direction he was taught as a child and to make it his own as an adult.

"The theological merits of these ideas are arguable, as students of church history can assure us, but on practical grounds I appreciate them very much. I never felt pressure from my parents to be holy. They didn't see every misdeed as proof that we were in need of conversion. Outside I got pressure being a preacher's kid, but never in my own home."

People respond to different things, of course, and some need gentle prodding toward godliness while others, like the apostle Paul, need stronger measures. "Still," writes Stafford, "I think it is reasonable to say that a child raised in a pastor's home is likely to know the gospel and to be aware of his need for a Savior. He rarely needs to have the lesson banged home. In fact, since nearly every teenage kid would do anything to avoid being an exact replica of his parents, pressuring him may make his decision much more difficult; to say no is the only way he can prove that he is an individual."

Another helpful principle is *to respect the individual's freedom of choice.*

M. O. Vincent saw this congenial control modeled by his father when it came time to choose between medical school and seminary. "Dad told me, 'If you feel you can do anything else except become a minister, and be satisfied, do it. I became a minister because I couldn't be satisfied with anything else.' "

The younger Vincent eventually opted for medical school and went on to become medical superintendent of a large psychiatric hospital in Ontario. His father demonstrated one of the key principles of parenting: offering direction while allowing the freedom for his son to grow and make crucial decisions.

As one Seattle pastor said, "Our children are loaned, not given to us, by God. We do our best to raise them to fear and love the Lord, but eventually we have to give them back to him. How they respond to God is not a total reflection on us. We do our best to be faithful, but we can't make their commitment to God for them."

For parents in the midst of difficulties with a straying child, perhaps the sustaining hope is that the final chapter has not yet been written. Parents trust that the One who authored the Prodigal Son's return will also pen their family a happier ending.

Indeed, based on the survey, there is cause for hope. Time and time again, parents spoke of their anguish as sons or daughters rejected everything the parents stood for. But an encouraging number of the stories wound up with an ending similar to this one:

"One of our four children rebelled. She had a difficult time accepting God's way, became a prodigal daughter, and eloped with another pastor's son. They lived in Hawaii; she threw away her Bible and avoided us. We *prayed* and *prayed*, continued to write her and send love gifts. After several years, she 'came to herself' and returned to a strong walk with God. She has moved back to our city and is a real blessing to us."

There are others, of course, who do not return — at least not to their parents' knowledge. These parents often struggle with feelings of failure. They're tempted to evaluate their worth by how their children turn out.

Ultimately, however, our calling to ministry and our worth as persons are not dependent upon the decisions our children make. The key is how faithful we are in raising our families and in responding to their decisions.

A pastor from Michigan put it this way: "It's a mistake to think, *I have to be a big success with my family so people will respect me.* To make our family's performance the foundation of our credibility is to put a load on them they may be unable to bear.

In fact, that pressure may contribute to their cracking.

"No, my role is to be a man of integrity and credibility, a man who is consistent at church and at home, a man who does his best to minister to both his flock and his family. If I do that, I've fulfilled my calling."

TWELVE

HOW THE FAMILY HELPS MINISTRY

*Dad was committed to Mom; the folks
were committed to the kids; our home
was committed to the Lord; and our
energies were committed to the church.*

PAUL D. ROBBINS

I asked a pastor's wife from Washington in what ways she contributed to her husband's ministry. "I'm the only person who can get him to church both happy and on time," she said with a twinkle in her eye. She's used that line to limit the number of church responsibilities she assumes. "I tell people that's such a big job that I have to let other people use their gifts in many of the other areas of ministry."

Family members contribute to the effectiveness of a ministry in a variety of ways. Even if they aren't directly involved in church programs, they still have a tremendous indirect impact. From the LEADERSHIP research, here are some ways family members help ministry.

A source of support. Many pastors testify to the sense of stability and support they gain from their families. "They encourage me; they believe in what I'm doing for God," says one pastor. "I think that's important. I want to be behind them in the same way in whatever they're doing."

A minister from Ohio says, "Spending time with the most important people in my life not only builds self-esteem, it also restores my energy and renews my vision. A healthy family life prevents my tendency to be consumed by the ministry and supplies love and encouragement from people who see me in terms of who I am, not what I do."

A measuring stick for ministry. Family members play a unique role in keeping ministry skills sharp. "Not only is my wife my best critic, but she has also, in a sense, become the goal of my ministry," says a pastor from Michigan. "As I evaluate my preaching, I ask, *Did I feed Martie this morning?* If so, I feel I've done my job. She's heard almost all my sermons. She also knows me, so she would know if my preaching did not match my practice. It's a great treat to hear her say, 'God really worked in my life today.' That's the ultimate compliment."

Ivory tower busters. Families help give a realistic view of life. One pastor said, "Since I've tried to limit my counseling, some people are unnecessarily alarmed: 'You don't counsel anymore; you're going to get out of touch with your people.' But as long as you have a real family in a real world, you're in touch with where your people are. You have job problems. You have to put gas in the car. Your kids get in trouble at school. It's the same stuff."

Family members can also be an excellent hedge against pomposity or self-pity. A Southern California pastor tells this story on himself: "One Sunday after the service, I came in and stood in the kitchen next to Chris and said, 'Can I help you with something?' She got me busy with some vegetables, and I said, 'Boy, I just don't know about today.'

" 'What are you talking about?' she asked.

" 'Oh, the message.'

" 'Honey, it was great!' she said. 'It spoke to my needs. It was really powerful.'

" 'Thanks, Dear.'

"Then, with a wry smile, she said, 'Is that what you were fishing for?' "

Sermon inspiration. Most pastors today also point to their families as a great source of sermon illustrations.

At one time, preachers were discouraged from being too

familiar or personal in their sermons. The feeling was that too much self-disclosure focused attention on the preacher and not on the Word being preached.

Peter Marshall, the renowned preacher and chaplain of the United States Senate, was greatly influenced by this attitude, but over time found his approach changing. One of Marshall's practices was to read his Sunday morning sermons to his wife, Catherine, on Saturday night. For him it was a warm-up; for her it was an enjoyable preview and a chance to offer input.

William J. Petersen, in *Catherine Marshall Had a Husband*, writes: "One Saturday night, as Peter reached the middle of his practice sermon, Catherine interrupted him. She hated to do it. But she had to tell him something important. She was having labor pains.

"Shortly before nine the next morning Peter John Marshall was born. Peter was at the hospital for his son's birth; then he returned to church in time to teach the young people's Sunday school class at ten and preach his half-rehearsed sermon at eleven. To his congregation he never said a word about the excitement that had occurred in his household a few hours earlier. Some people mentioned to him that he seemed tired that morning, almost as if he had been up all night. He still admitted nothing. Then as he was shaking hands with his parishioners at the close of the service, one woman asked him about Catherine, whom she had observed was absent that morning. Peter finally had to divulge the reason for Catherine's absence.

"It had always been a policy for Peter not to mention his wife or his home life in his sermons. After Peter John was born, however, that policy was quickly forgotten. Peter John provided too many colorful sermon anecdotes to be neglected."

Many preachers follow Marshall's lead and turn to the fertile ground of their family life for sermon material. This is, indeed, one of the benefits of having a family. But family illustrations are to be used with caution. Congregations can tire of them, and family members can be sensitive about the exposure.

One pastor's son wrote: "Being a preacher's kid can be embarrassing, especially if your father regularly uses you in sermon illustrations. The worst was when my brother and I starred in several hypothetical stories as well as true episodes told from the pulpit. To illustrate one point, my father created a story about the two of us shooting out the front window of a 7-Eleven with a BB gun. It never happened. I've never shot a BB gun. But to this day, most of the church people believe it really did happen. I dare say they forgot the point, but they didn't forget the illustration. I know I won't."

So most pastors take two precautions: (1) they get permission of their family members before mentioning them in a sermon, and (2) they don't use family members as negative examples. If an illustration makes a family member look good, it's a candidate, but if an example is needed of failure or shortcomings, pastors find it's better to use themselves — not family members.

"I don't reveal anything that hurts my relationship with my wife or my kids," said a Minneapolis pastor. "I use them most of the time to show how I was wrong and needed to learn something. For instance, I've told about the time when the kids were small and we were all in the car. They were restless, and I got so angry while driving that I turned around and swatted them hard. I used that as an example that, while discipline might have been needed, I was wrong in the way I did it, and I later needed to apologize to them even though they were small."

With these guidelines in mind, however, the family can be a source of enriched sermon material.

Enhanced outreach. Many pastors have found that family life provides opportunities for outreach. Simply being a parent provides an immediate point of common interest with other parents.

Mary Manz Simon, wife of Lutheran pastor Hank Simon, points out: "A number of people have met Hank because he's active in the public school where our children go — accompanying them on field trips, assisting as a tug-of-war captain on field day, talking to the class about his trip to Guatemala.

"For example, not long ago, we got a call from a lawyer we'd met through our children's school. I don't know if he's a Christian, but he was preparing for a trial against another lawyer who's known to quote lots of Bible verses. He asked Hank to help him find some biblical quotations on justice. So Hank prepared two pages for him. Later, the lawyer said he'd never thought of the issue of justice as a biblical concept and he'd begun spending time reading the Bible himself.

"And a mother met Hank because he often picks up the kids after school. She wasn't going to any church, but after meeting Hank, she came to church, was baptized, and now serves on the congregation's evangelism board. And each of our children has brought at least one family to the church." The family can provide natural avenues to tell other people about God.

Hank Simon also has taken one of his children along when he's making evangelism calls, initial contacts with church visitors, or passing out brochures about the church. "People who would never open a door for a man in a clerical collar will welcome somebody who's pushing a stroller or who has a 6-year-old kid with baseball cards," he says.

The Simons reflect the motto for their church: "A family sharing Christ." As Mary Simon says, "And what better way to illustrate that than to have a pastor going out on calls with his kids?"

An integrity check. Many pastors admit that family life helps keep them honest. An Indiana pastor confesses: "Once when I 'spouted off' at home, our son quietly asked, 'Dad, do you behave that way with the church board?' He had me. I knew I had to readjust my patterns."

A second way that families help maintain Christian integrity is described by Helmut Thielicke in a series of sermons, *How the World Began*, preached to a West German congregation in the middle 1950s. He said, "The Scriptures present the word of the Creator: 'It is not good that man should be alone.' It is not good, therefore, that he should be a self-contained organism which proceeds to develop itself; he must rather have a vis-á-vis, a partner, a companion, a thou. And here the Scripture touches on one of the fundamental mysteries of our life. It is remarkable — and this has become my personal conviction, confirmed at every step of the way by life itself — that I do *not* attain the greatest possible development of my personality when I consciously try to develop myself, when I am constantly considering, 'Where will I have the best chance to live life to the fullest? How can I reach the maximum accomplishment, and where can I experience the greatest pleasure?' On the contrary, I arrive at this fulfillment of my personality and my life as a whole when *I do not think about it at all;* but rather, when I forget myself and devote myself to someone else or something else."

As Thielicke knew, and countless other pastors have discovered, life lived to the full is life invested in others. Both family life and church life provide plenty of opportunities for such fullness. But while the temptation of church life is to see service as a profession, a role to assume, family life provides the antidote.

As another pastor on the survey said: "My family forces me to apply truth to life, and they provide a test tube for faith. That's where I find out if my own faith is affecting the way I live."

EPILOGUE

All the maxims have been written. It only remains to put them into practice.

BLAISE PASCAL

A recent LEADERSHIP cartoon shows a pastor's wife cheerfully saying to her husband, "I've got an idea! Let's switch things — today you can be grouchy at church and charming at home."

Most ministry families understand the cartoon's humor. The underlying premise is an example of what Paul Tournier has described as the difference between the "personage," the outward image we present to others, and the "person," that internal, hidden, deeper part of us. In ministry, the contrast is often seen in the way our words and actions are clothed at church — and the way they're bared at home.

You walk into the church on Sunday, and people immediately turn their heads your direction. They want a blessing, an opinion, or simply some warm attention. You make conversation, and people actually listen. You tell a funny story, and people laugh. People approach you in a steady stream, knowing you will graciously respond. People. People. People.

But too often at home, the kids hear, "Daddy's had a rough day. Let's be quiet." They vanish to another part of the house. There are no warm smiles, no requests. They've learned this is *not* the time to demand Dad's time and energy.

Why the difference between the effervescent public figure and the edgy private person?

Most pastors are genuinely ministry oriented. That's a key ingredient of their *person*. But so much sensitivity, compassion, and goodwill is expended in church work that the stores are depleted by the end of the day.

With some people, the personage clearly reveals the person. For most of us, however, especially if we must stand before a congregation made up of friends and strangers, supporters and critics, the personage and the person will always be somewhat distinct.

But while the personage is never a perfect reflection of the person, it can be a generally clear one. That allows others to understand our deepest dreams and convictions. It also allows our families to benefit most from our ministry; our public ministry then reinforces our private efforts to build a godly home.

Counselor James Hilt, reflecting on the personage versus the person, said, "Congruity is a good barometer of emotional and mental health. A split personality destroys not only emotional health but one's character as well."

Hilt suggests we pattern ourselves according to Jesus Christ's unconditional love, inner character, and firm commitment to God. He observed, "What if a casual observer of Christ would have approached Peter or John to ask, 'This Jesus character seems like a wonderful guy, but I know how celebrities are: you get close to them and the veneer vanishes. What's Christ *really* like?' The disciples likely would have responded, 'We have lived with him for years, and the more we see of him, the more magnificent his character becomes. What you have seen is real. But you have gotten only a hint of who he really is.' "

As pastors who are also parents, this is the challenge: to merge the person and the personage.

Pastor Chuck Smith, Jr., put it this way: "Our ministry in the pulpit is what we say; at home it's what we are."

As we commit ourselves to reshaping both our person and our personage, our goal is to enable those closest to us to respond like the disciples. If our wives or children are asked, "Your husband (or father) seems so solid, concerned, and kind. Is he really like that?" then they'll be able to say, "Yes, that's the real him. But you have seen only the surface of his deep, abiding love."